A R R O W

A Boston Mills Press Book

Published by Boston Mills Press, 2004
132 Main Street, Erin, Ontario N0B 1T0
Tel: 519-833-2407 Fax: 519-833-2195
e-mail: books@bostonmillspress.com
www.bostonmillspress.com

In Canada:
Distributed by Firefly Books Ltd.
66 Leek Crescent
Richmond Hill, Ontario, Canada L4B 1H1

In the United States:
Distributed by Firefly Books (U.S.) Inc.
P.O. Box 1338, Ellicott Station
Buffalo, New York 14205

National Library of Canada Cataloguing in Publication

Arrowheads.
Avro Arrow : the story of the Avro Arrow from its evolution
to its extinction / the Arrowheads. — Rev. ed.

Includes bibliographical references and index.
ISBN 1-55046-047-1

1. Avro Arrow (Turbojet fighter plane) I. Title.

TL685.3.A77 2004   623.7'464'0971   C2003-905312-1

Publisher Cataloging-in-Publication Data   (U.S.)

Arrowheads.
Avro Arrow : the story of the Avro Arrow from its evolution
to its extinction / the Arrowheads.
Revised edition. Originally published, 1980.

[   ] p. : ill., col. photos. ;   cm.
Includes bibliographical references and index.
Note: The Arrowheads is composed of four individuals:
Richard Organ, Ron Page, Don Watson, and Les Wilkinson.
Summary: The Canadian-built Avro Arrow, the most controversial fighter plane in history:
history, development, test flights and cancellation of the program with drawings, diagrams and photos.

ISBN 1-55046-047-1
1. Avro Arrow (Turbojet fighter plane). I. Organ, Richard, 1940- II. Arrowheads. III. Title.
623.7/464/0971 21   UG1242.F5A86 2004

Printed in Canada
Title page painting by Jan Stroomenberg

The publisher acknowledges the financial support of the Government of Canada
through the Book Publishing Industry Development Program (BPIDP) for its publishing efforts.

Avro Arrow

The Story Of The Avro Arrow
From Its Evolution To Its Extinction

The
Arrowheads

The BOSTON
MILLS PRESS

ACKNOWLEDGEMENTS

This book is not the result of four people but of many. We have included the names of some of the people who helped make this book possible.

Thanks to Colin Clarke, for help with both front and rear dust jacket photos, and a number inside...

A special thank you, must go to John Painter of Hawker Siddeley, Canada, who went out of his way to be helpful in our project and who made time in his busy schedule to try and answer yet another of our questions.

To Jan Zurakowski, Spud Potocki, Jack Woodman and Peter Cope for sharing with us their recollections....

To Mike Cooper Slipper for his recollections and experiences on flying the B-47....

To Jan Stroomenbergh, whose artwork graces the pages of this book and speaks for itself . . . .

To Ken Barnes and Mario Pesando, for helping us on accuracy; and to Jim Floyd who has helped us in too many ways to count, a very special thanks....

To Don Rogers, who has advised and checked our efforts in so many ways....

To Harry Keast, who remembered so much about the Iroquois.

Some contributions were small, others great, all were significant, none will be forgotten.

Peter Allnut	Bill Fitzackerly	Peter Martin	H.J. Samson
R.K. Anderson	Les Fraser	Hugh Mackechnie	Sam Schlifer
Burt Avery		Curly McBride	Fred Shortt
	Fred Gilbertson	Bill McDowell	Mrs. K. Shaw
Cliff Baskin	Arthur Gooch	John McGee	George Shaw
Chas. Batchlor	Don Gordon	Dave McKenna	Ray Simpson
John Beilby	Geoff. Grossmith	Lou McPherson	Stan Sivihila
Sheldon Benner	Bill Gunston	Larry Milberry	Fred Smye
Helen Bloor	Fred Guthrie	Alex Milne	Fred Stevens
Bob Bradford		Bill Morgan	Greig Stewart
Pete Brennen	Bob Halford	Ken Molson	Jim Stewart
Syd Britton	Tom Harrison	Pete Mossman	Dave Sugden
Bill Brimly	Jack Hilton	Doug Moore	George Szukala
Pete Brurrell	Ray Hooper		
Gord Bruce	Fred Hotson	Herb Nott	Ed Tabener
	Jack Humphreys	Ron Nunney	Tommy Thomson
Roy Cheeseman	Jack Hurst		Lauri Timlin
Russ Clarke		G.C. Palk	Doug Tough
Joe Corrigan	Ken Jay	Dan R. Perley	
Bill Coyle	Peter Jerden	Jack Phipps	Carl Vincent
	Frank Jessop	Peter Plant	
Frank Danby	Bob Johnson	George Proctor	Bill Wheeler
D.E. 'Red' Darrah		Joe Purvis	Don Whitley
Tom Dugelby	Justin Kilbride		Lou Wise
		John Reed	Nick Wolochatiuk
Chas. Erb	John Latremouille	Paul Regan	
	Don Laubman	Dave Roberts	Wray Youmans
John Farmer		Dave Robinson	Sid Young

CONTENTS

Acknowledgements   iv

Foreword   vii

Introduction   ix

Evolution of the Arrow   11

Design, Development & Construction   15

From Rollout to First Flight   35

Flight Test Program   57

The Log Book   113

Iroquois Engine & Flight Testing   121

Weapons System & Defence Strategy   133

Black Friday   139

Company Summary January-February 1959   151

Arrows for the Future   155

Technical Data & Drawings   163

Addendum – 30 Years Later   181

Bibliography   183

Index   184

FOREWORD

During the past year several papers, books and television programs have told and retold the story of Canada's outstanding achievement in aeronautical engineering, designing and manufacturing of the Avro Arrow aircraft and Orenda Iroquois engine.

This recent outpouring of historical reminiscences may have been generated by the fact that 1979 marked the twentieth anniversary of the complete cancellation of the projects or, perhaps, by the laudable endeavour to document these past events of Canadian aviation history before the details were lost in the haze of failing memories. In any case most of the writings have concentrated on the politics and personalities involved in the controversial decision, not only to stop the development and production of the aircraft and engine but also to destroy the five Arrows already flying and all others in various stages of construction together with all engineering drawings and plans.

While those accounts have made very interesting reading and undoubtedly sparked much thoughtful consideration of the problems associated with operating under combined industry / military / political contractual arrangements, the four authors of this book, the Arrowheads as they call themselves, decided to concentrate instead on the engineering, technical and flight testing aspects of the aircraft and engine. Their lengthy and exhaustive research has enabled them to present, for the first time, a remarkably detailed account of the Arrow and Iroquois from the early design concepts through the manufacturing to the complete flight test program and untimely termination. This book also includes a most comprehensive collection of photographs of the engine and aircraft and of many of the people involved and a fascinating look at some of the startling future development versions planned, had the program continued.

The Arrowheads have produced a work that I think will appeal to all who are interested in Canadian aviation history and, particularly, to those who may wish to read a detailed account of the design, manufacture and test flying of an aircraft and engine so advanced that their capabilities are only now being approached by the latest military fighter aircraft.

The authors have performed a very worthwhile task in having researched the subject so thoroughly and published the information in book form before the records were lost forever.

Donald H. Rogers

First 50 years of powered flight in Canada

1909-1959

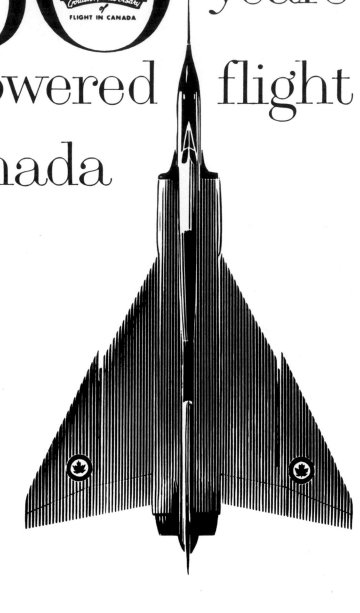

From the DART in 1909 to the Arrow in 1959 a pattern of aeronautical accomplishment has been dramatically recorded in Canada. The past half century of Canada's growth and increasing stature has been greatly accelerated by the swift and vigorous momentum of the men and machines of the Air Age.

Well established in the Jet Age, Canada's aeronautical resources will continue to meet the urgent requirements of a nation on wings.

AVRO AIRCRAFT LIMITED

MEMBER: A.V. ROE CANADA LIMITED & THE HAWKER SIDDELEY GROUP

INTRODUCTION

The history of the Avro Arrow is one of the most fascinating, yet misunderstood stories in all the annals of Canadian Aviation.

The Arrow was a plane without equal and considered by many to be twenty years ahead of its time.

In this book we will attempt to unravel some of the mysteries about the Arrow and expose the reader to some of its lesser known facets. We will take you from the Arrow's inception and early design studies, to roll out and from flight test to the advanced proposals for the development of future versions. We will describe and show by pictures some of the action behind the scenes. Photos of the Arrow were never widely circulated which explains why many aviation books simply omit the Arrow or give it cursory mention. This is understandable since cancellation of the Arrow called for destruction of all photos, drawings, models, specifications, tooling, etc.; even the aircraft themselves were destroyed. It is for this reason that photos, drawings, etc. that do exist are highly prized by the few collectors fortunate enough to have them.

We have gathered together what we feel is a good historical record of many previously unpublished photos and information. Statements in this book are based on fact and are all documented. Sources include taped interviews with the Test Pilots who give their firsthand impressions and interviews with various company officials and with countless plant personnel. We were indeed fortunate to have access to surviving company records and de-classified Government information. Our thanks go to many contributors and technical advisors who helped to put this information together to provide an accurate story. The politics of the Arrow have been written about many times and most people have formed their own opinions. We have no intention to repeat these arguments and ask that you read the book with an open mind.

In the following pages we wish to present to you the story of the Arrow —the airplane, not a political faux pas, but a page in the history of Canadian Aviation.

CF-100 Mark 5M, shown with Sparrow 2 missiles, carrying out trials for the CF-105 Arrow weapons system program.

The Evolution of the Arrow

Before the story of the Arrow can be told, we must step back into history to see why there was a need for such an aircraft in Canada. As it usually takes more than six years from concept to production, advance planning is essential!

In 1946, the Royal Canadian Air Force (RCAF) made the decision to re-equip its front line fighter squadrons with a two-place, long range, twin-engined, day and night, all-weather interceptor. An evaluating team of RCAF officers visited aircraft factories in the United Kingdom and the U.S. to ascertain whether there was an aircraft on the drawing boards, which could fill the requirements.

Apparently there was not and they persuaded the Canadian Government to take the momentous step of financing the design and development of a suitable aircraft in Canada. The CF-100 all-weather fighter was the result. This was designed and built by A.V. Roe, Canada, and was powered by Canadian engines of the Orenda series.

The outcome of this decision must be judged on the basis that, in addition to being the standard Canadian all-weather fighter with the North American Air Defence System (NORAD), the CF-100 was also in service with RCAF Air Division in the North Atlantic Treaty Organization (NATO). It was chosen, in a keen competition with other available types of aircraft, to re-equip the Belgian Air Force.

During the development of the CF-100, A.V. Roe had been looking at advanced versions of the aircraft even before the prototype had flown. One of these was the swept wing CF-100S of July 1948 with two Turbo Research (later Orenda) TR9 engines. In the summer of 1949, the main advance project became a CF-100 capable of supersonic speed, designated CF-100D.

With the expected decline of advanced engineering work on the CF-100, the company was in a position to employ its design team on this new study. In December of 1950, A.V. Roe made a submission on a swept wing version of the CF-100. They decided that this would be an interim weapon meeting part of the operational requirements in reasonable time. This aircraft was designated the CF-103 and preliminary estimates, made prior to the wind tunnel tests, indicated supersonic dive performance.

The Department of Trade and Commerce was requested to authorize A.V. Roe to proceed with the construction of two prototypes and one static test CF-103 aircraft. The better performance of the CF-103 as compared to the CF-100, and the use of the existing CF-100 fuselage, made the aircraft a logical development of the CF-100. It was considered a good interim aircraft between the CF-100 and the designated C-104 advanced fighter. The estimated first flight of the CF-103 aircraft was July 1952. By February 1951, detailed engineering and tool design had been started, as well as the high speed wind tunnel testing, to check performance estimates. This testing was done at Cornell Aeronautical Laboratories in Buffalo, New York, since no high speed wind tunnels were available in Canada.

Manufacturing of jigs, tools and details started in June 1951. The first flight was rescheduled from July 1952 to June 1953, when increased engineering and shop work on CF-100 Mark 3 and Mark 4 were given priority, necessitating the setting back of the CF-103 program.

Wind tunnel tests were completed and analyzed in November of 1951, indicating that the aircraft would probably not dive supersonically, without considerable development that would involve further wind tunnel tests. These same results indicated that there was some doubt that the aerodynamic limitations on top speed could be overcome with the proposed configuration. This, together with the fact that the aircraft's proposed first flight would be delayed until at least June 1953 and therefore the aircraft would be obsolete before it could be produced in quantity, resulted in

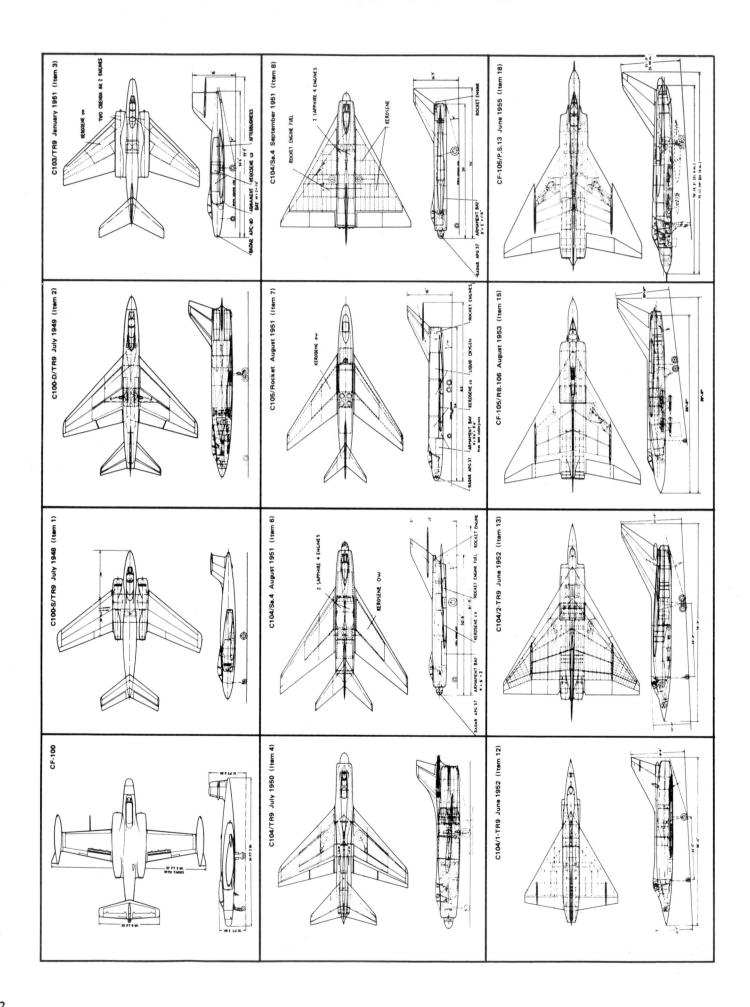

C103/TR9 January 1951 (Item 3)

C104/Sa.4 September 1951 (Item 8)

CF-105/P.S.13 June 1955 (Item 18)

C100-D/TR9 July 1949 (Item 2)

C105/Rocket August 1951 (Item 7)

CF-105/RB.106 August 1953 (Item 15)

C100-S/TR9 July 1948 (Item 1)

C104/Sa.4 August 1951 (Item 6)

C104/2-TR9 June 1952 (Item 13)

CF-100

C104/TR9 July 1950 (Item 4)

C104/1-TR9 June 1952 (Item 12)

the cancellation of the CF-103 program in December 1951. The priority was therefore raised on the proposed C-104 advanced fighter.

In 1950, the advanced project group of A.V. Roe had not been idle and had produced several new ideas that were submitted to the Canadian Government: the C-104 powered by two TR9 engines, with a crew of two and a cannon. There was also a radical aircraft powered by a liquid oxygen-kerosene rocket, which weighed 20,000 lbs. This proposal had a wing area of only 600 sq.ft. and was designated C-105. The small rocket project stayed alive until 1951, and included in this submission was a delta wing version.

The general arrangement of the aircraft and studies mentioned in the previous paragraphs give a history of how the Arrow project was generated. These proposals were studied by the RCAF and they came to the conclusion that the requirements of 1950 should be replaced, because approximately one year had elapsed since the requirements had been specified and a re-study had indicated a rapid advance in the "state of the art."

In January of 1952 an "All Weather Requirements Team" had been formed at Air Force Headquarters to re-study the new operational requirements for an advanced fighter. On receipt by A.V. Roe of the recommendations contained in the "Final Report" of the "All Weather Interceptor Requirements Team" in March 1952, A.V. Roe submitted two more brochures to the RCAF in June of 1952.

These brochures described two superb delta aircraft in considerable detail; one for a single engined aircraft designated C-104/1, the other for a twin-engine designated C-104/2, both intended to meet the conditions laid down by the Requirements Team. The advantages and disadvantages of each of these proposals were also pointed out.

The RCAF seemed to be in favour of the twin-engined proposal, so A.V. Roe continued its studies in this area.

In April 1953 the RCAF issued Specifications Air 7-3 "Design Studies of a Prototype Supersonic All-Weather Aircraft" to A.V. Roe for the purpose of selecting the optimum aircraft capable of meeting RCAF Operational Requirement OR1/1-63 "Supersonic All-Weather Interceptor Aircraft". The new RCAF specification requirements were staggering and surpassed anything documented in any other country in the Western world.

The specification called for a fighter which could operate from a 6000 ft. runway, have a range of 600 nautical miles, be capable of accelerating to Mach 1.5, have a crew of two and carry a very advanced type of missile with a control system capable of operating in Canada's harsh environment, yet still be able to manoeuvre at 50,000 ft. while pulling 2G. The new weapons system and missiles required that the aircraft have a weapons bay larger than the bomb bay of a B-29 Bomber. In the meantime, an evaluation team, led by Wing Commander R. Foottit, was again sent out to the countries in the Western Alliance, to search for a suitable inteceptor. Again it was decided that none of these countries had a project, either in design or contemplated design, which fully met the Canadian requirements.

Because of the peculiar Canadian Defence requirements, the non-availability of a suitable weapon elsewhere, and the ability to meet the Canadian requirements that had been demonstrated by an established Canadian aircraft industry, once again the decision was taken to design and develop a fighter aircraft in Canada.

Even though it is jumping ahead in time, it is interesting to note that Foottit's examination team looked at the F-101 Voodoo fighter in the U.S.A. during their searching tour, and quickly decided that it fell short of their requirements. They could not have realized that this would be the aircraft that would be issued to the RCAF after the Arrow project had been cancelled and scrapped.

To meet the AIR 7-3 requirements, A.V. Roe concentrated on a two seater version of the designated C-105. It had already been established that the high wing delta was a good basis to work on because this configuration gave good access to the engines and a large weapons bay. To determine the optimum aircraft to best satisfy the demands of the specifications, a range of wing areas were studied and tested, from 1,000 sq.ft. to 1,400 sq.ft. and designated C-105/1,000 to C-105/1,400. The final selection was the C-105/1,200 having a wing area of 1,225 sq.ft. This design and other proposals were presented to the RCAF in May 1953. It took only a short time for the Air Force to agree, that the C-105 was what they were looking for.

In July 1953, a ministerial directive was issued from the Department of Defence Production authorizing the design study of an aircraft to meet AIR 7-3. Preliminary design on this aircraft was given the project number CF-105, which was the real start of the Arrow project.

CF-103 wooden mock-up

Overall view of restricted area showing extra cockpit framework (left), and complete extra cockpit (right) engine is shown on stand and was used to obtain dimensions for cowlings, etc.

Completed view of mock-up without undercarriage

Design, Development and Construction

To treat the design of the Arrow in one chapter is an impossible task; it would really take a whole book. We have summarized the subject and created a section at the end of the book, showing various drawings of some of the major components of the aircraft and its vital statistics.

The first step in the design study, was to adapt the concept to Rolls Royce RB 106 engines, which were then in an advanced stage of development. The first wind tunnel tests on models were run in September 1953 — only two months after the government gave the go ahead. The wind tunnel models were tested from low speed to twice the speed of sound.

The low speed tunnel at National Research Council (NRC) Ottawa, was used. Avro used more sophisticated facilities in the U.S.A. including high speed model testing at Cornell Aeronautical Laboratories, Buffalo (New York), in the transonic range, and supersonic testing of model sizes at National Advisory Committee for Aeronautics, (NACA) facilities, Langley Field (Virginia). Other NACA facilities were used at Lewis Laboratories, Cleveland (Ohio), for air intake tests. Over seventeen models were used, ranging in scale from 1/80 to 1/6th.

Due to wind tunnel limitations, Avro used a program of free-flight models, fired on Nike rocket boosters. This was to simulate supersonic speeds of the full scale aircraft at high altitudes. Eleven free-flight models were fired, nine from Point Petre, (near Belleville, Ontario), and two in the U.S.A. at NACA range in Virginia. All rocket launchings were successful and good data was recorded.

In 1954, after preliminary design was complete, the RCAF adopted the CF-105 designation for the aircraft. Initial proposals, design studies and tests which led to establishing the basic configuration of the CF-105, were mainly due to the efforts of the preliminary design office, under the direction of Jim Chamberlain, who became Chief of Technical Design.

Later in 1954, powerplant problems arose which required major changes to the aircraft. The Rolls Royce RB106 engines would not be available in time for the CF-105 and were replaced by two Curtiss-Wright J67 engines. Then, in early 1955, the U.S. Air Force disclosed that the J67 program was being discontinued. Avro turned to the problem of installing Pratt & Whitney J75s as an interim measure, until the Orenda PS13 (Iroquois) would be available. Although the Iroquois development was well advanced, and its specifications more than met Avro's requirements, the combination of an untried engine and a new air frame was considered too risky.

A great deal of theoretical work on the application of the "Area Rule" was carried out on the CF-105 project. This method of refining the fuselage shape to give the so-called "Coke-Bottle" effect was used to reduce the supersonic drag of the aircraft.

Both the RAF and the USAF were kept constantly informed of the progress of the Canadian project, and contributed significant encouragement by their concurrence in the soundness of the design.

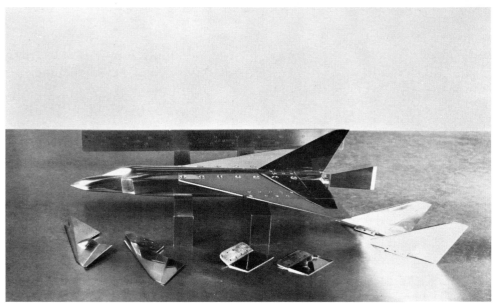

Small wind tunnel models showing various components

Wind tunnel model under test showing missiles extended

MODEL TESTING PROGRAM

MODEL	PURPOSE	FACILITY
	(a) WIND TUNNEL	
3/100 COMPLETE MODEL	STABILITY & CONTROL (SUB & SUPERSONIC)	CORNELL 3' x 4' AND 10' x 12'
4/100 COMPLETE MODEL	STABILITY & CONTROL ARMAMENT FORCES (SUB & SUPERSONIC)	CORNELL 3' x 4'
1/10 & 1/8 REFLECTION PLANE	ICING CONDITIONS (LOW SPEED)	N. A. E. 10' x 5.7'
7/100 COMPLETE MODEL	CANOPY & MISSILES JETTISON, GROUND EFFECTS (LOW SPEED)	N. A. E. 10' x 5.7'
1/80 COMPLETE MODEL	STABILITY & CONTROL (SUPERSONIC)	N. A. E. 16" x 30"
1/40 FUSELAGE INTAKE	INTAKE FLOW (SUPERSONIC)	N. A. E. 10" x 10"
1/50 REFLECTION PLANE	STABILITY & CONTROL (SUPERSONIC)	N. A. E. 16" x 30"
1/24 COMPLETE MODEL	SPIN CHARACTERISTICS (SUBSONIC)	N. A. E. SPINNING TUNNEL
1/6 FUSELAGE INTAKE	INTAKE STUDY (SUB & SUPERSONIC)	NACA CLEVELAND 8' x 6'
3/100 COMPLETE MODEL	DIRECTIONAL STABILITY (SUPERSONIC)	NACA LANGLEY 4' x 4'
1/50 CANOPY MODEL	RAKE SURVEY (SUBSONIC)	N. A. E. 10" x 10"
1/10 COMPLETE MODEL	FLUTTER (LOW SPEED)	N. A. E. 10' x 5.7'
1/40 REFLECTION PLANE	FLUTTER (TRANSONIC)	M. I. T. 22" DIA.

MODEL	PURPOSE	FACILITY
	(a) WIND TUNNEL (CONT'D)	
4/100 FIN MODEL	RUDDER BUZZ (SUPERSONIC)	N. A. E. 16" x 30"
4/100 COMPLETE MODEL	MISSILE TRAJECTORIES, CANOPY HINGE MOMENTS AND STABILITY EFFECTS (TRANSONIC)	CORNELL
$\alpha - \beta$ VANE FULL SIZE	FUNCTIONAL TESTS (SUPERSONIC)	N. A. E. 16" x 30"
	(b) WATER TUNNEL	
3/100 CANOPY MODEL	VISUAL FLOW CHECKS (LOW SPEED)	N. A. E. 9.84" x 13.11" WATER TUNNEL
	(c) ENGINE DUCT MODEL	
6/10 DUCT MODEL	FLOW, EFFICIENCY AND AIR BLEED TESTS	ORENDA TEST CELL
	(d) FREE FLIGHT MODELS	
1/8 SCALE FREE FLIGHT (11 MODELS)	DRAG & STABILITY (SUPERSONIC)	C.A.R.D.E. RANGE ONTARIO AND LANGLEY FIELD RANGE
	(e) ANTENNA RESEARCH	
1/48, 1/18, 1/8, 1/10, .07, AND FULL SCALE MODELS	ANTENNA & ANTENNA PATTERN RESEARCH	SINCLAIR RADIO LABS. LTD.

MODEL TESTING CHART

Engineering mock-ups of the full aircraft were built to provide a three-dimensional check on installation clearances and general accessability. The first was mainly of wood with some metal formers, while a metal mock-up was built later. Numerous changes were required in the engine bay structure to accommodate the J75s in place of the original J67s engine. The RCAF evaluation of the wooden mock-up took place in February 1956, and included assessment of a metal mock-up of the weapon pack.

To demonstrate pilot visibility while taxiing and cockpit lighting techniques, a special mock-up of the front cockpit was mounted on a truck to simulate the actual height and attitude of the cockpit during taxiing. This mock-up was later modified to include the radar nose and the trials were repeated.

Early in 1956, the engine bays of the mock-ups were modified to accommodate the Iroquois engine and its installation was investigated. Again later in the year, conversion of the remainder of the engineering mock-ups from CF-105 Mk 1 to CF-105 Mk 2 configuration began. A number of ground support equipment mock-ups were also built for design appraisal.

The CF-105 was officially designated the Avro Arrow in early 1957 and the two versions of the aircraft designated Arrow 1 and Arrow 2.

Aerodynamically, the Arrow was entering a new realm of science. Performance, stability and control problems were difficult to evaluate, and data had to be obtained to establish airloads on the wing, fin, canopy and control surfaces. In this respect, wind tunnel results proved and supplemented theories in overcoming some of the

Large free flight model

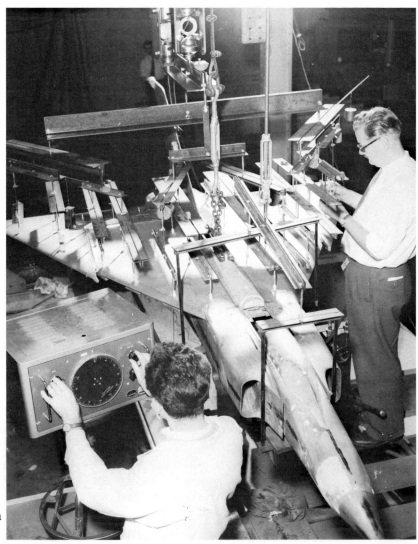

Structural test of a free flight model with strain gauges to measure deflections

Large free flight models mounted on Nike rockets. Free flight models were used in early development stages of the Arrow, to gather aerodynamic data.

Static test aircraft

Dummy being lowered into static aircraft to test Martin-Baker ejection seat (1958). In an actual test the seat was ejected upwards and backwards, its trajectory being determined by the length of the retaining cable. The cable eventually came into contact with a cross-bar, fitted between two sixty foot towers, causing the seat to be flipped over into a net.

problems. Improvements in longitudinal stability, buffet characteristics, subsonic drag and directional stability were a direct result of wind tunnel testing.

The Arrow structure was designed to provide a high wing delta planform. Due to this new shape, the high performance and the effect of manoeverability on the structure, a large number of stressing tests had to be carried out.

Tremendous power is required to fly an aircraft at supersonic speeds and the Arrow used as much power as that taken to drive two ocean liners, the size of the Queen Mary. To provide this power, the engines consumed fuel at the rate of more than a quarter of a ton per minute. Much of this power would be dissipated in air friction at these very high speeds. This friction raised the aircraft skin temperature to such a high degree that a problem arose that had not previously been explored.

Temperatures experienced while flying supersonic were high enough to weaken the structure — the higher the speed, the higher the skin surface temperature and that of the whole aircraft. Air conditioning was required to protect the crew and electronic equipment. This system on the Arrow had the capacity to produce twenty-three tons of ice a day.

Another problem was caused by sound. There were two main types of sound that could effect the structure — jet engine and aerodynamic, and these caused skin panels to fracture and rivets to loosen. Tests were done continually until re-design demonstrated a satisfactory life of the panel or structure.

The Arrow development presented some undreamed of problems, compared to those encountered when the CF-100 was designed. At supersonic speeds, airloads on the control surfaces are extremely high, and the pilot must be provided with considerable amplification of his physical strength in the form of control mechanisms. Those installed on the Avro Arrow were strong enough to lift the equivalent of six elephants standing on the elevators.

In modern military aircraft such as the Arrow, elaborate electronic systems are required. These systems in the Arrow required eleven miles of wiring and enough vacuum tubes to equip two hundred television sets.

The Arrow, from the onset of design and construction, was to be built from production tooling, which was a radical approach compared to hand built prototypes of the past. The primary objective of this approach was to get the aircraft into production as soon as possible, and hence into squadron service in the shortest possible time. This procedure was known as the Cook-Craigie plan in the U.S.A. but had yet to be applied to such a complex and advanced aircraft program as the Arrow. Therefore to minimize the risks involved in an operation of this type, extensive testing of all structures and systems was required, before the production drawings and tooling could be released to build the first aircraft. Some tests were minor, others, such as the fuel test rig, were more complex. This fuel system rig simulated in its operation, any position the aircraft may take in its flight and could investigate the pressures and flow characteristics under normal and abnormal conditions. The functional testing of all the major and minor aircraft systems before the aircraft flew would reduce expensive and time consuming airborne testing to a minimum, and once again shorten the time taken to get the aircraft into squadron service.

The first Arrow would take only 28 months from the release of the first drawings in June of 1955 to roll out in October 1957. By going directly to a production aircraft instead of a prototype, cost savings were enormous. The cost per pound in producing the first Arrow was in the neighbourhood of 15 to 20 man hours per pound, whereas 25 to 40 were normal under previous methods. When this saving in man hours is multiplied by the aircraft airframe weight (20 tons), the results were spectacular compared to the old construction methods. This type of approach produced two other advantages which are worth noting — the first Arrow weighed in with an error of only 62 pounds compared to the estimated weight; and the center of gravity was within 0.25% of the estimated position.

One of the best features of the Arrow was the ease of converting it to a number of different roles, due to its large and easily exchanged armament bay. The bay was three feet high, eight feet wide and eighteen feet long, larger than the bomb bay of the B-29 Bomber. An armament pack could be hoisted up into the belly of the aircraft and attached at four points. It was also possible to put into these packs a variety of equipment including extra fuel tanks, and possibly bombs. It made the Arrow a very neat and tidy aircraft, compared with the vast array of equipment hanging underneath the wings of most modern aircraft, attempting to carry out the same role.

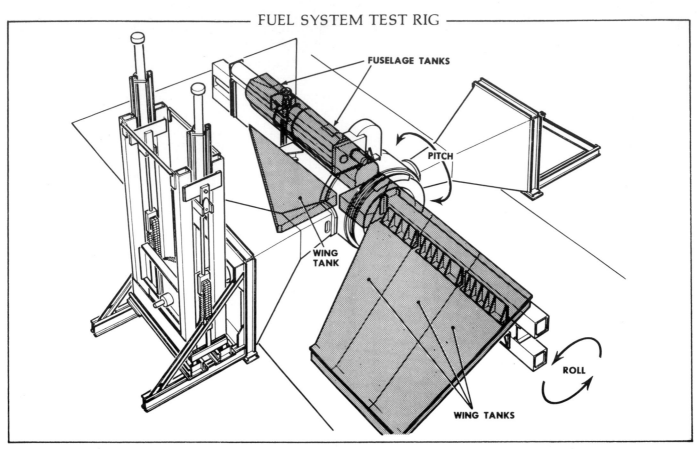

Integral fuel tanks were a feature of the Arrow. Extensive checking of the whole system was continually carried out on this specially built test facility.

Extensive testing was carried out on this static test aircraft, including the application of 100% load limits by weights attached to the aircraft.

The electrical system test rig could simulate, exactly, the complete electrical system of the aircraft. Any production electrical component could be checked for servicability on this rig.

A mockup of the cockpit was mounted on a truck at actual height and taxiing attitude of the Arrow in order to check pilot visibility under actual daylight and night operating conditions.

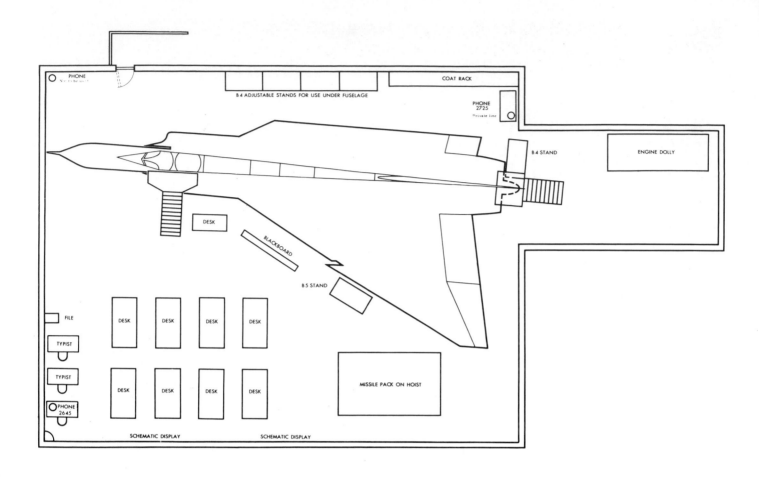

Floor plan of wooden mock-up area

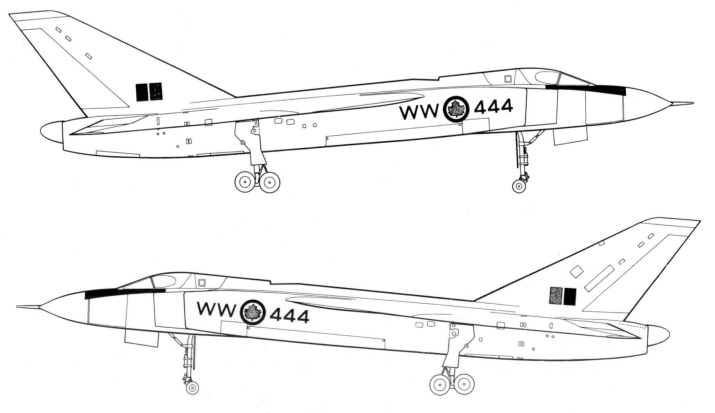

Early wooden mock-up drawing

Early photo of wooden mock-up showing J-75 engine fit check.

View of mock-up showing engine being installed

More completed wooden mock-up (CF-206) showing crane in position to enable photographer to photograph pilots and observers cockpits

Pilots cockpit — wooden mock-up, showing clamshell canopy fully open

Wooden mock-up, Observers cockpit

Weapons pack showing method of installation. Pack was placed on dolly which was wheeled to position under aircraft. Four cables were then attached to aircraft fuselage (clearly seen in photo, above dolly wheels, dolly is already clear of floor), man is shown operating dolly control panel; dolly and pack are both hoisted up to aircraft, pack is attached at four points to aircraft, and dolly is then lowered back down to floor to detach hoisting cables.

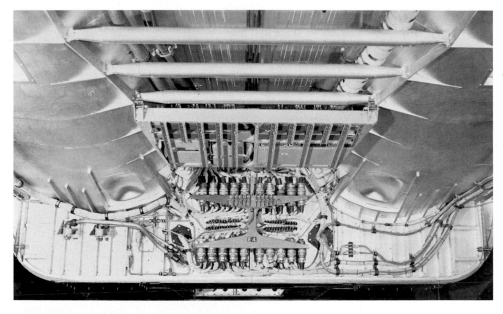

Mock-up of the weapons bay showing extensive piping and wiring

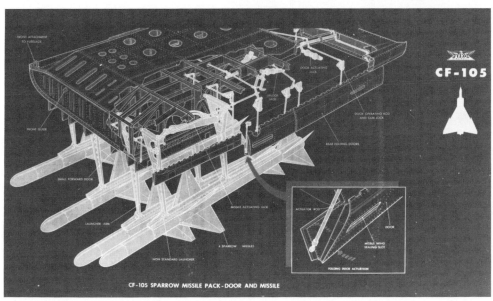

Arrow weapons pack with Sparrow missiles extended

Metal mock-up in early stages of construction showing unfinished fuselage area and identification stencil on wing

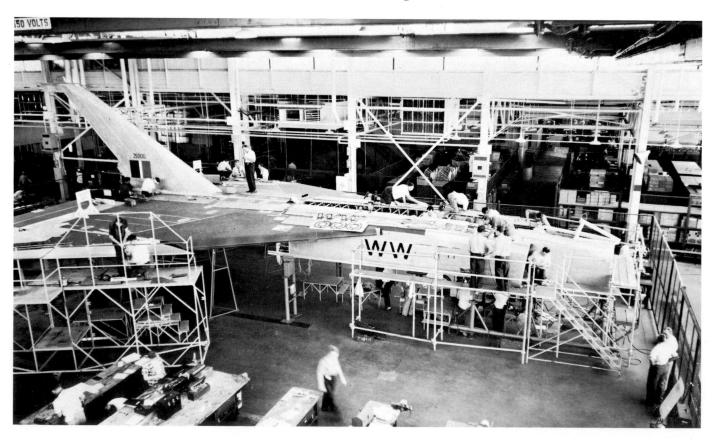

Metal mock-up (early)

Mock-up showing start of production line to the rear

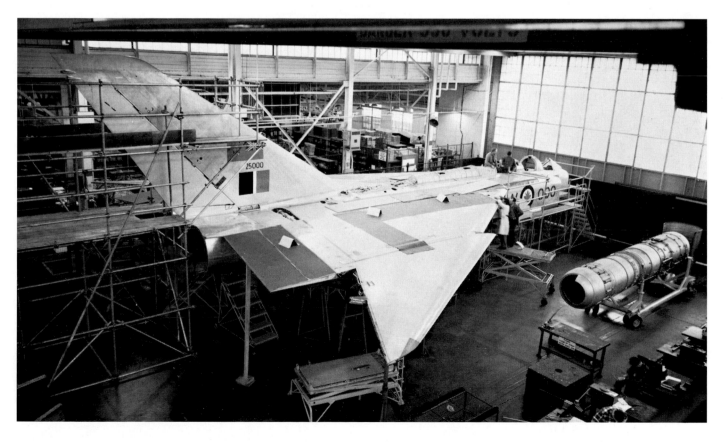

Metal mock-up nearing completion, ready for dummy engine fitting

Arrow 201 — initial stage of construction showing delta wing platform

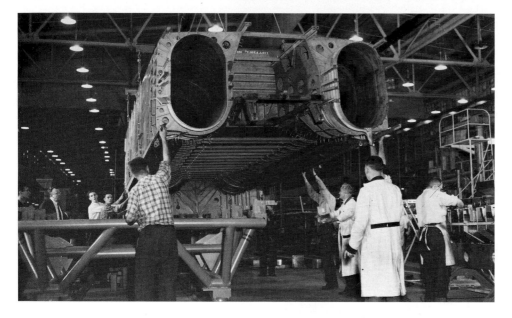

Fuselage centre section — the key section for Arrow number one is shown being lowered onto its marry-up handling trolley for transfer to main assembly jig.

Engine enclosure being lowered onto trolley for installation to main delta platform

Initial stages of final assembly — skins riveted onto centre section; inner wings have been installed

Marry-up of cockpit section to main fuselage section of first Arrow

Partly completed aircraft being moved, on rails, to next assembly point

Aircraft at new location,
clear of rails

Rear view showing engine
tunnels. Aircraft is now
ready for installation of outer wings.

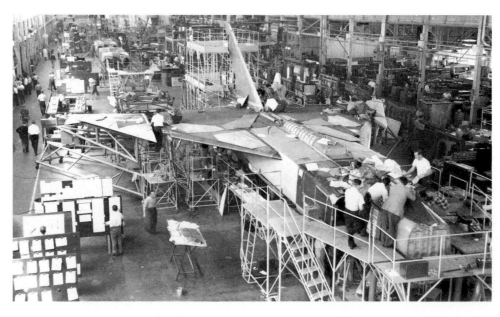

General view of the first Arrow, final assembly, as seen from metal mock-up.

The four men who co-ordinated the efforts of all phases of engineering which went into creating the Arrow. (L. to R.) R.L. (Bob) Lindley, Chief Engineer; J.C. (Jim) Floyd, Vice-President Engineering; Guest Hake, Arrow Project Designer; and J. (Jim) Chamberlin, Chief Aerodynamist.

From Roll Out to First Flight

The official roll out of the Arrow on October 4th 1957 was the same day the Russians launched their famous Sputnik! This relegated the Arrow to a secondary importance in the media.

The unveiling ceremonies culminated what had begun some six years earlier as the germ of an idea in the minds of a small group of creative engineers, headed by J.C. (Jim) Floyd — Vice-President Engineering, and made up of: R.N. (Bob) Lindley, Chief Engineer; Jim Chamberlin, Chief Aerodynamist; and Guest Hake, Arrow Project Engineer. These four co-ordinated the efforts of all phases of engineering which went into creating the Arrow. The supersonic delta concept was not new, but these people felt it was possible for Canada, through engineering and production facilities of Avro, to design and produce in quantity an advanced aircraft type to meet the threat of future developments of potential enemy bombers.

About 12,000 people viewed the roll out, including representatives of Military, Government and Industry from NATO countries together with as many Avroites as could possibly be spared from their work for the period of the ceremony.

The Honorable George R. Pearkes V.C.,

Minister of National Defence, unveiled the ARROW with these words: "I now have the pleasure of unveiling the AVRO ARROW — Canada's first supersonic aircraft — a symbol of a new era for Canada in the air."

The following is an excerpt from his address:

"Fifty years ago a great Canadian pioneer, John A.D. McCurdy, who is with us on the platform today, flew the Silver Dart, the first aircraft in Canada, in fact it was the first heavier-than-air plane to fly in the British Commonwealth. History recognizes that event as the beginning of Canada's air age.

"This event today marks another milestone — the production of the first Canadian supersonic airplane. I am sure that the historian of tomorrow will regard this event as being equally significant in the annals of Canadian aviation.

"The supersonic era of flight is just beginning. Many of today's aircraft are regularly breaking the sound barrier, but this is done at the extreme peak of their performance. Supersonic flight is still not a routine matter. Present aircraft travel at these

October 4th, 1957. Roll-out, first official debut of the Avro Arrow

Crowd reaction, as the Arrow comes into full view, has spectators standing on their seats.

exceptionally fast speeds for a relatively short period of time.

"The Avro Arrow, however, has been designed from the outset to operate supersonically throughout as much of its mission as is deemed necessary. It will be as equally at home at one side of the sound barrier as on the other. It will be a truly supersonic aircraft.

"It is difficult for the layman to appreciate the magnitude and complexities of the problems of the last four years culminating in this first phase of the Arrow project. Four years ago the Air Force and the industry set out together on a voyage into the unknown. All the technical difficulties which have been solved thus far have represented pioneering work in aerodynamics, metallurgy, mechanics and electronics and in all the related arts and sciences which form part of our aeronautical industry. Thus far, progress has been commendably rapid.

"We are, of course, only part way along the road and no-one would be so foolish as to suggest that the job is complete by any means.

"Four years of designing, testing, tooling and production problems lie behind. Many months of further tests, trials, complex development and modification lie ahead before this aircraft can be considered operationally acceptable. I understand it will be some years yet before this supersonic aircraft with its missile and guidance systems will be available for operational use. We are looking forward to this time.

"It is important to appreciate the significance of proper timing in the introduction of weapons under today's conditions. Our weapons must not only be designed to be better than those of unfriendly nations, they must be ready in time to counteract those weapons should the need arise. If either the timing is wrong or the quality is wrong, we fail to maintain the proper balance of power in our goal towards presenting the most effective deterrent.

"I would like to recognize the great number of Canadians in our industry who have contributed towards this project. I would also like to thank the personnel of those American agencies who have helped so materially in the aircraft's development. As the Chief of Staff said, the development of the Arrow has been an outstanding piece of co-operation between the Service and Industrial agencies on an international level.

"Much has been said of late about the coming missile age and there have been suggestions from well-intentioned people that the era of the manned aeroplane is over and that we should not be wasting our time and energy producing an aircraft of the performance, complexity and cost of the Avro Arrow. They suggest that we should put our faith in missiles and launch straight into the era of push-button war. I do not feel that missile and manned aircraft have, as yet, reached the point where they should be considered as competitive.

"They will, in fact, become complementary. Each can do things which the other cannot do, and for some years to come both will be required in the inventory of any nation seeking to maintain an adequate "deterrent" to war. However, the aircraft has this one great advantage over the missile. It can bring the judgment of a man into the battle and closer to the target where human judgment, combined with the technology of the aircraft, will provide the most sophisticated and effective defence that human ingenuity can devise.

"The aircraft now being produced in the various countries of our NATO alliance may or may not be the last of the manned interceptors. With the rapid strides being made in the fields of Science and Engineering, it would be unwise to attempt to forecast the future in this respect. However, I feel sure that if these aircraft continue their development with the same promise as they have in the past, there is no doubt in my mind that they will be a necessary requirement to the arsenal of the West for man years to come.

"In closing, I would like once again to commend the efforts of those who contributed thus far to the development and production of this airplane. Through your efforts you are making a direct contribution to the defence of the free nations of the world and so to the well-being of us all."

The future, looking at the future!

Tow away from roll-out

Tow away from roll-out

Arrow pauses for official photograph

'Fuelling up'

Arrow being positioned for engine runs; CF-100 also on engine test

Vapour clouds rise from water-cooled mufflers during engine testing. It was necessary to tether Arrow during these tests especially with afterburners in operation.

Ground Running and Low Speed Taxi Trials Commenced

On Wednesday, December 4th, 1957, engine ground running began with Arrow 201. The first part of this program was conducted in very cold weather and the man in the cockpit appeared to be the only one happy about the whole thing. The bellow of the J-75s from the direction of the run-up base was to become a familiar sound. Six engine run-up noise reducing units were installed along the taxi strip leading to the rolling gate. Officially, they were known as the "Durastack muffler installation." Three of the units had special adaptors which could be moved into place for ground running of the Arrow. Water was injected into the jet stream to cool the muffler when the afterburners were operating causing clouds of steam. It was prudent to keep well away from the rear of the aircraft. The danger area extended to 100 feet with the engines at idle and increased to 350 feet with maximum afterburning. With afterburners in operation the jet efflux 100 feet behind the aircraft was moving at 200 knots with a temperature of 400 degrees F.

Both engines were run together for the first time December 18th, 1957, when Jan Zurakowski (Zura), Chief Experimental Pilot, completed the engine runs.

By January of 1958, low speed taxi trials had commenced and Zura had made six taxi runs up to speeds of 100 knots. He felt that the aircraft was very easy to keep on the runway and that the engines were behaving themselves very well. The low speed trials had been highly successful, although some trouble was experienced with the operation of the drag chute. The chute was operated on five occasions, but as three of the releases were unsuccessful, modification to the release mechanism was required.

By January 3rd, the engine tests and low speed taxi trials had resulted in a running time of 9 hours (approximately) on each engine. After the low speed taxi trials were completed, the aircraft was taken back into the hangar to be given a thorough check over in readiness for the second phase of taxi trials leading to first flight. Both engines were removed and the flight control system hooked up to the simulator for further tests. The right hand engine flow control unit was replaced and the engine reinstalled, the other engine was reinstalled on the completion of the simulator testing. It is appropriate to note at this point that in a report made by Zura on the earlier taxi trials he said that "a negligible amount of engine power was required to get the big aircraft moving and idling thrust was sufficient to keep the speed in the 25-50 mph range." Single engine taxiing was reported to be good, and Zura recommended that it be used after landing, to conserve fuel. Successful streaming of the drag chute at 100 knots stopped the aircraft in 7,000 feet with only light brake application. Another interesting sidelight of the ground runs then completed, was the use of a special paint to check the thermal conditions in the engine bay area. Thermindex oil-resisting, temperature-sensitive paint was applied to the structure around the engines, jet pipe etc. It was claimed by the manufacturer to be accurate within 15 degrees C. The paint colour changes were irreversible and required no instrumentation. Further applications were used for temperature readings on other pre-flight engine runs and for the determining of brake drum temperatures during high speed taxi trials.

On the armament side, many preliminary tests were carried out on the weapons pack front seals, and the telescopic links of the missile extension gears, to check wear characteristics. Operation of the missile doors were tested and dummy missiles fired into a barricade of sandbags to determine launcher rail wear. The Iroquois engine used during the Arrow 2 mock-up conference was returned from Orenda after having had minor modifications incorporated. A trial installation of the modified engine was also made in the wooden mock-up. During the mock-up demonstration to show engine installation, an Iroquois was removed from the aircraft and replaced in less than thirty minutes.

High Speed Taxi Trials

High speed taxi trials were commenced and the parachute brake was getting a thorough workout as a new improved method of deployment was being used. It was a familiar sight during these times to see the Arrow racing along the runway with the chute streaming out the rear as it approached the end of the runway. It was during these trials, that the nose wheel door under extreme crosswinds, caused the aircraft to veer towards the down wind side of the runway. To combat this problem, the door was changed, so that it could be closed with the leg still extended. Brakes were also a problem. Since the brakes were designed, at the beginning, on the assumption of lower total aircraft weight and speed, they were

Taxi trials

Taxi trails with drag chute deployed

Jan Zurakowski, Avro's Chief Experimental Test Pilot, climbs into cockpit to take Canada's supersonic Arrow MKI onto the runway for the first time under its own power, for taxi tests.

Jan Zurakowski in cockpit of Arrow simulator, hooked up to an anologue computer, is assisted by fellow experimental test pilot 'Spud' Potocki while simulator supervisor Stan Kwiatkowski and members of his staff watch.

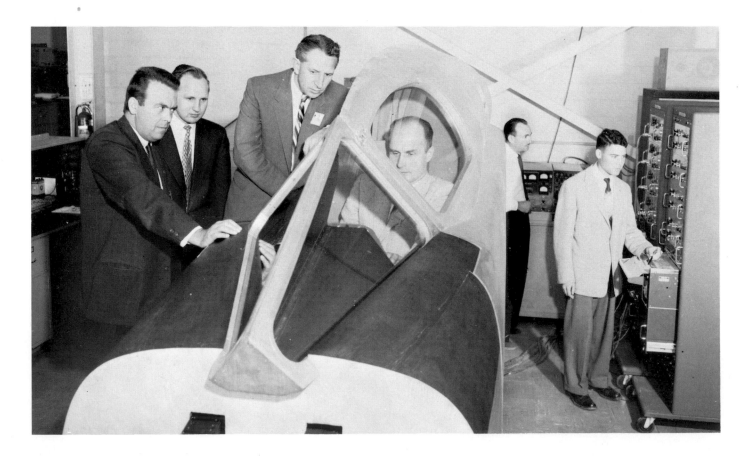

therefore inadequate and had to be changed. The braking kinetic energy of the aircraft was increasing the temperature of the brakes, causing the drums to actually change from red to white hot. This heat was transferred to the rims and caused the tires to burst.

To quote Zura on this problem, "There were a few cases when after taxi tests or after landing, I had to get out of the aircraft quickly and run as far as possible, stop and wait for four bangs — this told me all four main tires had exploded. It was then safe to approach the aircraft. This problem was of course rectified with a brake modification."

While all this was going on, the test pilots were being checked out on the flight simulator. The simulator was a masterpiece of workmanship. All the mechanical control systems were coupled to the largest computer in Canada at that time. The computer was fed all the aerodynamic parameters, height, speed, inertia of the aircraft, etc., to set up a condition to see how the pilots could handle the situation. According to the simulator, the aircraft was unflyable, as Zura obtained only short survival times. Spud Potocki, Avro Ex-

perimental Test Pilot, was a little better on the simulator, his survival time was about 8 seconds, but he got it up to 13 seconds after some experience. After talking over the low survival rate, Jim Floyd asked Zura what he thought. Zura said that he thought things would straighten themselves out, as he had flown 'so-called' unstable aircraft earlier in England and survived.

Shortly after this, they quit the simulator and started flying the real aircraft. After flying the Arrow, they went back and fed the simulator new derivatives for the control systems, it then worked flawlessly, becoming a major tool in the Arrow's development.

First Flight March 25th 1958

As the taxiing trials were just about completed and first 'take off' for the Arrow was drawing closer, considerable interest was being generated. The exact date of the first flight was, of course, unpredictable as it depended on many factors, not the least of which, was the weather.

As any experimental test pilot will testify,

Final taxi test prior to first flight

First flight take-off nose gear off

First flight. Arrow becomes airborne for the first time.

good weather and aircraft serviceability rarely coincide. However, at Toronto's Malton Airport, March 25th, 1958, both the Arrow and the weather were ready!

This day was about to become significant in Canadian Aviation History. The day started out much like any other day. The weather was fairly good with hazy sunshine through a high layer of thin cloud. First flight fever was running high throughout the Avro plant, just as it had the previous Saturday, when a hydraulic leak had caused the scheduled first flight cancellation. Just before 10.00 a.m., the P.A. system announcement was made, inviting all non-essential personnel to leave work and witness the first flight of the Arrow.

The plant emptied even faster than at normal quitting time! Jan Zurakowski had inspected the Arrow, RL25201, signed acceptance of it from the ground crew, and was ready to go! The watching crowd was tense as Zura climbed the somewhat tall boarding ladder, eased himself through the open clamshell canopy and down into his seat. A quick assist from his ground crew with strap-in, and all was ready for engine start-up. Engine start was normal and, with flight clearance, Zura quickly taxied the Arrow out to take-off hold position, at the south end of Malton's recently extended and longest runway, #32 (320°), 11,050 feet in length.

Meanwhile two chase aircraft had taken off and were awaiting Zura's signal that he was ready to take off. Flight Lieutenant (F/Lt) Jack Woodman, the resident RCAF Central Experimental and Proving Establishment (CEPE) Test Pilot, on the Arrow project, was flying the single seat F-86 Sabre. Avro experimental Test Pilot, "Spud" Potocki was flying a CF-100 with Avro photographer Hugh MacKechnie in the back seat.

Having obtained flight clearance, Zura moved the Arrow onto the runway and started to roll. The two chase aircraft, with flaps down, were approaching flying parallel to take-off runway. With terrific acceleration, the Arrow was quickly airborne, less than half way along the runway. History was recorded by Malton Control tower, "Avro 201 off at 9.51 a.m. and cleared to company tower." The take-off was without afterburners and the aircraft climbed steeply to around 5,000 feet with gear down, at an indicated air speed of 200 knots. At 5,000 feet the automatic flight control system (A.F.C.S.) was selected in the normal mode and the landing gear retracted.

At Zura's request, Spud Potocki, flying the CF-100 chase aircraft, closed in to ensure positive closure of the nose wheel landing gear door, as the uplock warning light was showing red in the cockpit. The speed was then boosted to 250 knots and the Arrow climbed to 11,000 feet where handling assessment was made with A.F.C.S. in emergency mode. For over half an hour, the Arrow flew around accompanied by the two chase planes. They kept very close to the Arrow and acted as extra pairs of eyes on the outside of the airplane, as Zura put the Arrow through a set of mild manoeuvers to check the response of the controls, engines, undercarriage and air brake operation, handling at speeds up to 250 knots and low speed in a landing configuration.

Zura later recalled that the aircraft flying characteristics were similar to that of other delta winged aircraft, like the British Gloster Javelin and American F102, but the Arrow had a more positive response to control movement. The only unpleasant part of the flight was the feeling of responsibility combined with the realization that the success of the flight depended upon the thousands of components, especially electronic and hydraulic, with only a small percentage under his control.

Zura obtained clearance to land, from Malton Control Tower, and the landing gear was lowered. The Arrow lined up with the runway and after a very fast descent with air brakes out, made its approach at 180 knots. The wheels touched — right on the runway button — at 160 knots. The tail parachute billowed and filled, slowing the aircraft until it turned off at the far end of the runway.

The aircraft taxied back through the entrance to the Avro Plant, was parked and the engines shut down. Zura climbed back down the boarding ladder and a large crowd which had gathered around the Arrow, lifted him shoulder high.

The gesture was a fitting tribute to the Arrow and to the masterful flying of the man who had first tried its wings.

The flight which had commenced at 9.51 a.m. was completed just before 10.26 a.m. and logged at 35 mins. The whole first flight was excellent with no major snags; only two microswitches had failed to work. The engineering department justly proud, had the first flight snag sheet framed.

Zura had only one other complaint, there was no clock in the airplane for him to see the time!

Maiden flight of the Arrow

Arrow 201 over Malton Airport (Toronto International Airport)

Arrow over Avro Aircraft's Plant on first flight

Approach for landing from first flight, air brakes extended.

Landing 'Roundout' first flight

'Touchdown' after successful first flight

Jubilant 'Avroites' hoist Jan Zurakowski onto their shoulders after the historical flight.

'Zura' and happy ground crew after flight

Photographic Coverage

A great many people have commented on the excellent coverage provided by the Avro Photographic Department on the first flight of the ARROW.

To obtain comprehensive photographic records of the flight, fourteen camera stations were located on and around the airfield, as shown on the map. The photographic equipment assigned to each camera station is described in the accompanying key. In addition, a photographer armed with two 16mm motion picture cameras and two still cameras was aboard the CF-100 chase plane, who obtained some fine air-to-air records.

F/Lt. Jack Woodman, C.E.P.E. Test Pilot, flying the F86 Sabre chase plane, was also engaged in photography, of a rather interesting method similar to that used during U.S.A. flight testing of the B-58 Bomber. A 16mm movie camera was mounted on the pilot's fibreglass helmet. Sighting of the camera was achieved by attaching a piece of masking tape to the helmet visor, the tape forming a vertical frame, giving 25° horizontal and 33° vertical view. Tests showed that results were fairly good and the method left both of the pilot's hands free to fly his aircraft. Other tests

Jack Woodman RCAF; in F86 Sabre Chase plane, shown wearing movie camera mounted on his helmet. This was used during flight test program.

indicated that the helmet/camera could be worn for periods up to 1¼ hours without becoming oppressive. In addition to this, Jack also operated a wing tip gun camera and cockpit gunsight camera.

CAMERA LOCATIONS

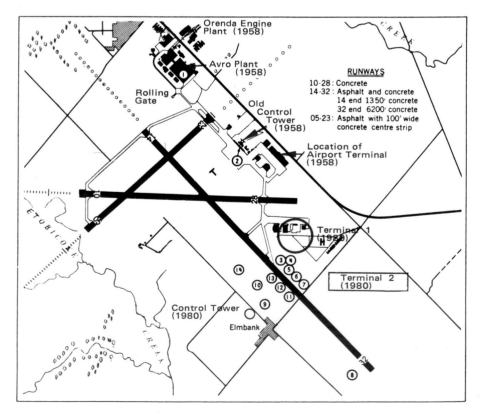

1	16 mm. motion picture camera
2	70 mm. Vinten take-off analysis camera
3	4 x 5 Speed Graphic
4	4 x 5 Speed Graphic
5	5½ x 5½ K24 sequence camera
6	4 x 5 Speed Graphic
7	4 x 5 Speed Graphic
8	16 mm. motion picture camera
9	70 mm. Vinten take-off analysis camera
10	16 mm. motion picture camera
11	5½ x 5½ K24 sequence camera
12	4 x 5 Speed Graphic
13	4 x 5 Speed Graphic
14	16 mm. high speed motion picture camera with a standard 16 mm. camera riding piggyback - both on one tripod mount.

Flight Test Program

A Few Words On The Arrow Flying Control System

During the flight test program there are many references to the flying control system and the various modes in which it could operate. Spud Potocki describes the overall system, later in the chapter 'Fly-By-Wire', it only requires a simple summary here with the definition of the three control modes. The Arrow's flying controls were fully powered, irreversible with artifical feel. There were two independent hydraulic circuits feeding the controls, each powered by two engine driven pumps. This system which operated the ailerons, elevators and rudder consisted of mechanical, hydraulic, electronic and electrical components. The pilot had no direct mechanical actuation of the control surfaces.

There were three modes of control: normal, automatic and emergency.

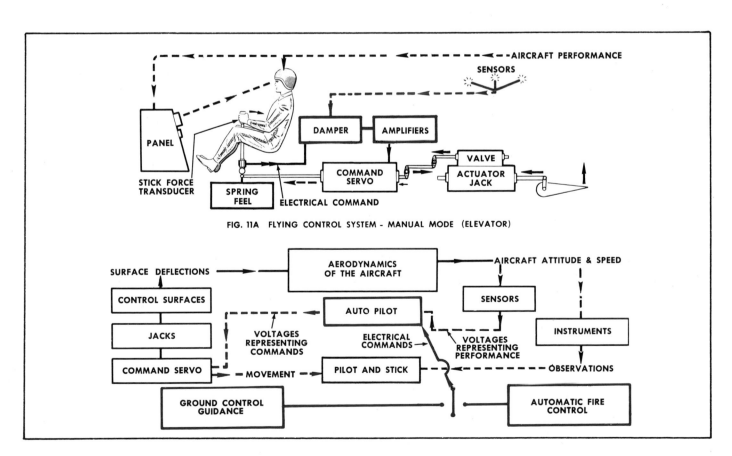

FIG. 11A FLYING CONTROL SYSTEM - MANUAL MODE (ELEVATOR)

BLOCK DIAGRAM OF FLYING CONTROL SYSTEM — AUTOMATIC MODE.

The Arrow's Flying Control System Modes

Normal Mode

When the pilot exerted a force on the control column to move the control surfaces a force transducer incorporated in the control column transmitted electrical signals to a series of servos, which converted the electrical signals into mechanical movement by means of hydraulic pressure. The movement of the control column followed the movement of the control surfaces. The response of the system was nearly instantaneous, and therefore it appeared as if the control column was being moved by the pilot. In this mode the damping system automatically stabilized the aircraft in all three axes.

Automatic Mode

The damping system would be operated as above, but elevator and aileron position would be controlled by automatic flight control system (A.F.-C.S.). This mode allowed the aircraft to be controlled from the ground. It was then called automatic ground control interception (A.G.C.I.). In this condition the pilot could hold a set course or altitude automatically, as well as maintain a selected Mach number by varying the pitch attitude of the aircraft. Automatic navigation was also possible by feeding information into the dead reckoning computer of the aircraft. The mode also made possible automatic ground control approach (A.G.C.A.). A disconnect switch was installed in the control column handgrip. This system mode was not fitted to the original early aircraft.

Emergency Mode

In this mode, the hydraulic components for elevators and ailerons, were controlled mechanically. Yaw stabilization and rudder co-ordination were maintained by an emergency yaw damper system.

If certain flight conditions were exceeded, the system automatically changed to emergency mode.

Pilot's feel on the control column was provided by the damping system in normal mode and by spring feel in the emergency mode.

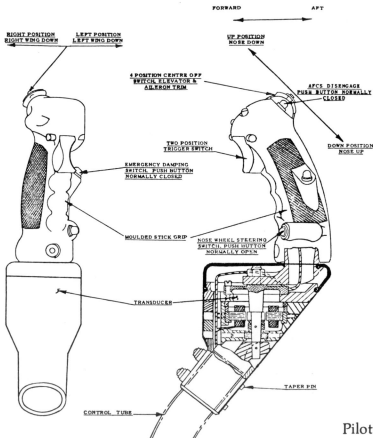

Pilot's control column handle showing automatic flight control buttons and switches.

First Phase

The first phase of the flight testing was intended to check the handling of the aircraft and the functioning of its systems. With the success of the maiden flight, the flight test program began. The initial testing took place in the general area between Toronto and Hamilton, in Southern Ontario.

The second flight of #201 took place during the early evening of Tuesday, April 1st, 1958. The program for this flight included a maximum indicated speed of 400 knots and a maximum altitude of 30,000 feet, but due to the nose wheel landing gear door not completely closing, the flight was limited to 250 knots. During the climb to 30,000 feet, Zura selected afterburner and headed upwards at an angle of 45 degrees at an indicated rate of climb of 6,000 feet per minute. The Arrow reached 30,000 feet at 250 knots, with a Machmeter reading of 0.65. During descent the aircraft was put into a 2.5G turn. The landing was made in semi-darkness and was so smooth that the recorder in the instrument pack did not register the contact of touchdown.

On the third flight, made on the morning of April 3rd, #201 flew to supersonic speed for the first time. This flight was made to assess the aircraft handling qualities at higher speeds and altitudes. After climbing to 15,000 feet at an indicated air speed of approximately 400 knots, the afterburners were lit and the Arrow climbed at great speed. Nearing 40,000 feet, Zura decreased the angle of climb and shortly afterwards the aircraft passed through the transonic region to reach Mach 1.1. As it was not the intention that the Arrow should go any faster on this flight, Zura then throttled back. Eventually the chase planes caught up with the Arrow and the three aircraft descended to about 2,000 feet to make a spectacular pass over the airfield. The chase aircraft peeled off and the Arrow, after another impressive climb with afterburner lit, joined the circuit and landed.

On the fourth flight of #201, made on Tuesday, April 15th, satisfactory telemetering of instrumentation was maintained for the first twenty minutes. The failure of a ground power supply stopped further reception of data, even though the airborne telemetry system continued to radiate good signals.

Zura took up #201 for its fifth flight on the morning of Thursday, April 17th, and climbed with afterburners on. The aircraft was put through a series of manoeuvers for photographic purposes and angle of attack measurements.

Both the sixth and seventh flights of #201 were made on Friday, April 18th. During the sixth flight, there were reports from the Hamilton area of the Arrow causing doors and windows to rattle. Late that same afternoon as Avro workers left the plant to go home, many of them parked their cars alongside the road so they could watch the vapor-trails at approximately 50,000 feet in the sky above the plant. The contrails were made by the Arrow. It was later announced by the RCAF that on this seventh flight the Arrow had achieved a level flight speed "equivalent to 1,000 miles per hour." The Arrow had achieved a speed of Mach 1.25 and Mach 1.52 was achieved at 49,000 ft. while the aircraft was still climbing. Following this flight, F/Lt. Jack Woodman, made a high speed taxi run in the Arrow and at one point lifted the nose wheel off the ground, but did not attempt to take off.

Testing of a supersonic military aircraft over Southern Ontario was something of a new experience to the local residents, and complaints started to be heard within an approximate 50 mile wide corridor, coinciding with the area of the Arrow's flight at that time. As a result of these complaints, the flight testing corridor was moved further North over less populated areas. A quick check of the flight record shows that the Arrows created sonic booms on about 47% of the total test flights (31 out of 66).

On the afternoon of Tuesday, April 22nd, #201 was flown by f/Lt. J. Woodman, the RCAF acceptance pilot and the only RCAF pilot to fly the Arrow. This flight was mainly one of familiarization, although some tests were made on the A.F.C.S. The Arrow attained a speed of Mach 1.4

Spud Potocki, the Avro Experimental Pilot, took #201 up on April 23rd on its ninth flight, the last flight to be made in this phase.

The first Arrow had completed its first phase of test flights and had made nine flights in the first twenty-nine days of flying; it had generally achieved a high degree of reliability. The Arrow then went under minor modifications and further instrumentation was incorporated before the next stage of test flying was started.

The following is an extract from a detailed report by Jan Zurakowski on the handling qualities of the Arrow based on his seven flights up to this time, with a total of 6 hours 30 minutes flying, (the end of the first phase).

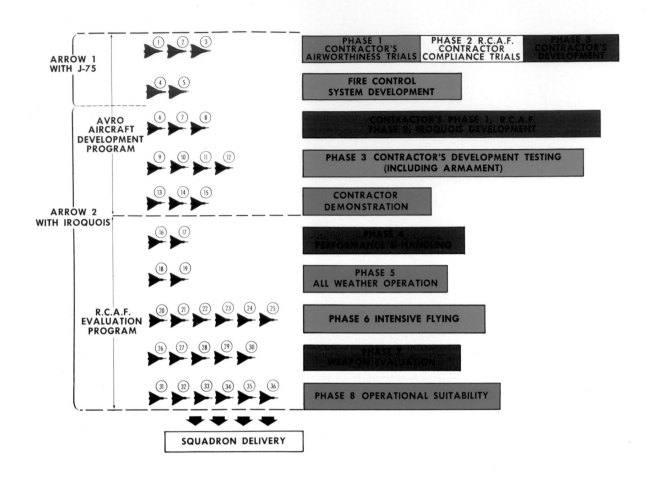

	PHASE 1 CONTRACTOR'S AIRWORTHINESS TRIALS	PHASE 2 R.C.A.F. CONTRACTOR COMPLIANCE TRIALS	PHASE 3 CONTRACTOR'S DEVELOPMENT

ARROW 1 WITH J-75

FIRE CONTROL SYSTEM DEVELOPMENT

AVRO AIRCRAFT DEVELOPMENT PROGRAM

CONTRACTOR'S PHASE 1, R.C.A.F. PHASE 2, IROQUOIS DEVELOPMENT

PHASE 3 CONTRACTOR'S DEVELOPMENT TESTING (INCLUDING ARMAMENT)

CONTRACTOR DEMONSTRATION

ARROW 2 WITH IROQUOIS

PHASE 4 PERFORMANCE & HANDLING

PHASE 5 ALL WEATHER OPERATION

R.C.A.F. EVALUATION PROGRAM

PHASE 6 INTENSIVE FLYING

PHASE 7 WEAPON EVALUATION

PHASE 8 OPERATIONAL SUITABILITY

SQUADRON DELIVERY

Arrow 201 take off (old wooden Toronto Flying Club hangars in background).

Gear retracting after take off.

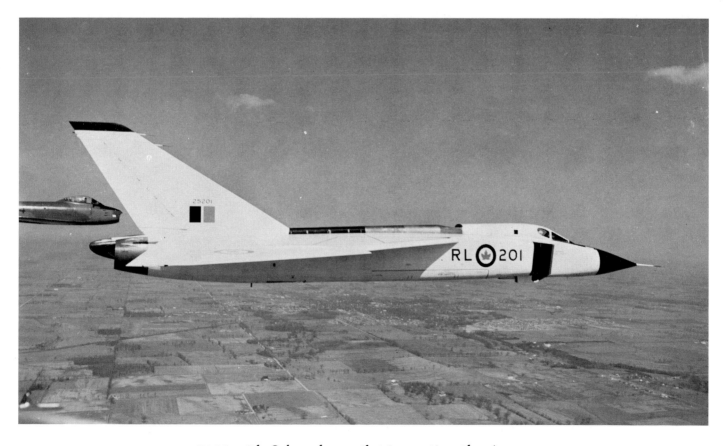

#201 with Sabre chase pilot inspecting the Arrow.

CF-100 chase aircraft follows close as Arrow lands.

Arrow in steep climb with afterburners in operation.

Jan's Impressions of the Arrow's Flying Characteristics - Conclusions

1. In general, handling characteristics and performance of the aircraft agreed well with estimates.
2. Take-off, initial climb, and handling at low speeds (limited by 15 degree incidence) were satisfactory. Some longitudinal pitching at medium speed were eliminated after first flight by alterations to elevator control circuit and, in the last flight, longitudinal behaviour of aircraft was much better. Speeds up to 450 knots ASI and turns up to 2½ 'G' were tested at low altitude. Lateral and longitudinal control was sensitive, and the pilot's tendency to over-control was present.
3. In flight no. 7 at 49,000 feet, aircraft reached Mach 1.52 on climb, still accelerating, showing excess of thrust available. Handling of the aircraft at supersonic speeds at high altitudes was good.
4. Landing characteristics of aircraft were satisfactory except that, apparently due to restriction of pilots view ahead, landing speeds were higher than estimated. Drag chute reliability was high, deceleration power very good.
5. Engine control was very good, reliability high, some loss of thrust at transonic speeds at higher altitudes was investigated.
6. The yaw A.F.C.S. system was a considerable help in accurate flying of the aircraft.

J. Zurakowski. (signature)

Second Phase

The second phase of the flight program had the objective of obtaining further data, primarily on stability and control problems using manual and damping inputs; also to evaluate the revised flying control system; to investigate the brake and gear dynamics; to define engine performance deficiencies and to evaluate the revised air conditioning system.

The vertical descent velocity just prior to touchdown was also to be measured by means of a movie camera mounted on the underside of the fuselage and focussed on the nose landing gear. A light attached to the leg was shone downward and immediately prior to touchdown, the spot of light showing on the ground came into view. From the time scale of the film, the undercarriage-to-ground closing speed was measured, The main gear was similarly lighted and photographed on the same film via angled mirrors.

An electro-hydraulic nose steering system, as opposed to the cable-operated system fitted to aircraft #201, was installed on the second Arrow aircraft RL25202, which was doing taxi trials by this time. The third Arrow RL25203, was to be used to cover Contractor Compliance Trials, and an Avro designed auto observer was installed in this aircraft to record air speed, r.p.m., temperatures, pressures, and fuel quantities. This auto observer was fitted into the armament pack and consisted of a camera, focussed on a bank of instruments to record readings during the flight.

From the standpoint of flying, there was no real difference between the Arrows. It was only in the test equipment required for the specific tests being made that they varied. Since each Arrow improved upon its predecessor, it was expected that with such high performance aircraft there would be many problems. In order to get over the experimental development as soon as possible, it would be logical to use a large number of aircraft. No longer was it possible to rely on one or two aircraft like in the old days, when there were prototypes and then preproduction aircraft. It would be impossible with only a couple of aircraft to check things like armament, radar, automatic control etc. with an aircraft as complex as the Arrow. Therefore each one was instrumented for special development as part of the test program. Telemetry had the capability of recording up to 200 different functions on the Arrow, and without it, it would have taken five or ten years to prove the aircraft's capabilities. Gone were the days of a pad on the Test Pilot's knee with long detailed discussion on the ground after each flight and the examination of films. With the Arrow, the engineers on the ground could watch the results of test flights as they occurred and instruct the pilot to continue to the next test or stop and return to base.

Damper trouble and a nose undercarriage door which stuck in the down position marred Arrow 201's 10th flight on June 7th.

Some of the test flights went smoothly, others showed signs of trouble. An example of this was the flight on which Zura had problems with polarity reversal on the A.F.C.S. sensor. This acceleration polarity reversal gave him magnified wrong responses shortly after take off. He quickly got things under control, otherwise he would not have survived due to the violent divergent motion which the A.F.C.S. was giving him, in opposition

#201 peels away from CF-100 chase aircraft.

Arrow 201 in flight

to what was required. It was, in fact, making it an almost uncontrollable aircraft, until Zura took over manually after disconnecting the automatic flight control system.

The Arrow was not too far into its second phase of testing when an incident occurred on Flight 11.

The Failure of the Undercarriage on Flight 11 — Arrow 201

The aircraft took off on Wednesday, June 11th, 1958, just after 2.00 p.m. and after a normal check flight of approximately one and a half hours, it landed on runway number 32. There was a very slight crosswind of 10 to 15 miles per hour N.W. The aircraft touched down on the strip at the extreme landing end of the runway extension. The parachute was deployed immediately on touchdown, and it opened during the first 1,000 feet of the landing run.

The aircraft gradually veered off the runway to port (left) at a point 4,000 feet from touchdown, at which time the port undercarriage dug into the soft shoulder, swung the aircraft around to port, snapping off the three gear units in the process. The pilot, Jan Zurakowski, was unhurt. This happened about 3.40 p.m.

A brief summary report outlining the sequence of events during the investigation of the accident and the speed at which they occurred is as follows:

The Investigation:

4.30 p.m.: On examination of the tire marks made by the aircraft during landing, it was found that the bogie on the port undercarriage gear had not rotated correctly to landing position.
5.00 p.m.: A meeting of Avro, and later, Dowty representatives (manufacturers of the gear) was held in an attempt to pinpoint the possible cause of leg malfunction.
6.00 p.m.: During the discussion, it was obvious that the only way the wheels could become staggered, to make twin tracks on the runway, was for the final action of the undercarriage mechanism, i.e., to lengthen and twist the undercarriage into line, had not, in fact, taken place. This was confirmed at 6.30 p.m. when close sequence photographs of the landing were made available showing that the bogie was twisted and not in the fully extended position prior to landing.

The aircraft had obviously touched down with the port leg incorrectly rotated and had been in this condition during the whole of the 4,000 foot run.
7.00 p.m.: Three possible causes of malfunction were defined:
(1) There could have been a failure in the chain which operated the leg extension mechanism and lock.
(2) There could have been a failure of the extension cam rollers, causing a jamming during extension, and
(3) There could have been a failure in the leg backing pawls. Since all of these were buried deeply inside the leg, the port leg was taken to the Experimental Hangar for examination prior to carrying out x-ray tests.
8.00 p.m.: Examination of the leg had shown that there was a distinct possibility that during extension the operating chain had become jammed between the main leg fitting and a debris guard. This could have been caused by the chain becoming slack during rapid extension of the gear, and then getting trapped. Marks on the debris guard appeared to confirm this, and it was looked upon as the most likely cause of the accident.
8.45 p.m.: A modification was suggested for the second aircraft which prevented the trapping of the chain and ensured that any slack would be internally within the leg in a safe area.
11.45 p.m.: The port leg was taken over to the Metallurgical Laboratory to be x-rayed.

In the meantime, the aircraft was being returned to the hangar, and arrived there early in the morning of Thursday, June 12th.

Thursday, June 12th

9.00 a.m.: The x-ray results became available and, on examination, they did not indicate the mechanism was in the unlocked position, unless damage had taken place either on the pawls or on the locking fitting. It was therefore decided to try and dismantle the leg without disturbing the lock. Dowty representatives thought that this could be done. The leg had been badly damaged, however, and the extension lock driven into the main leg casing with great force. It was realized that it would be difficult to sort out which was primary and which was secondary damage.
11.00 a.m.: Commencement on the dismantling of the leg.

A cursory examination showed that damage to the aircraft was fairly local, and was confined to the areas damaged when the undercarriage was ripped off, and to the rear end of the fuselage as the aircraft settled, fully on its "belly".

The main damage appeared to be in the nosewheel bay, where structural damage had occurred at the bulkhead framing members for the undercarriage pick-up and door, and at the port main wing-undercarriage fitting adjacent to the notch. These appeared to be extensively damaged, and their replacement would be a major job.

The port wing tip had been damaged and similarly the rear end of the fuselage had light damage affecting all the formers at the rear end. There appeared to be no damage to the engines!

The wing upper skins had to be cut open in order to lift the aircraft from the runway.

After this cursory examination, it was estimated to be at least 90 to 100 days before the aircraft would be flying again. (The aircraft was flying on October 5th, 1958, four months later, after repairs and modifications were made.)

Close up view of main landing gear showing complexity.

In Retrospect

.....In discussions with Jan Zurakowski, we asked for his impressions of the #201 incident....."Upon landing I suddenly realized that the aircraft was pulling to the left and that I could not maintain direction. Suspecting that the braking parachute did not open evenly, I jettisoned it; there was no immediate improvement, and at about 30 mph. the aircraft left the runway." On investigation it was established that the left undercarriage leg did not complete the lowering cycle and during the landing run the wheels were at about a 45° angle to the direction of travel. This produced a higher drag on the left side than the power of the brakes on the right could handle. At low speed, the rudder became ineffective and could not prevent the aircraft from changing direction.

"This accident was due to a technical error; first, part of the system failed to work correctly, and secondly, there was no warning light to show that there was trouble of this type. I had no indication that the undercarriage bogie was in the wrong position."

.....When asked why he didn't raise the undercarriage as the aircraft left the runway..... "Things happened fairly fast and you must realize that the aircraft was pretty heavy, being about thirty tons at the time. The tires were about 250 psi to 270 psi which is really a solid tire. Since the runway work had only been completed a short time before, the soil at the sides was quite soft with a light covering of grass on it. As a result, the tires dug in as soon as the aircraft left the concrete and the undercarriage could not stand the rapid deceleration, and it collapsed. Had things been normal and the soil at the side of the runway been hard, I possibly could have stopped the aircraft without any damage at all."

"This accident probably could have been avoided, had there been warning lights to indicate that the undercarriage bogie had not lined up correctly, or had a chase plane pilot watched during the landing sequence. The pilot could have alerted me, so that I could have landed slightly across the runway to allow for an expected constant swing to the left after touchdown. Hopefully I could have kept the Arrow on the hard surface of the runway. Unfortunately, both chase plane pilots had run low on fuel and had landed ahead of the Arrow."

We have gone into considerable detail on this incident, not for sensationalism but to clear up many of the misleading statements made about it.

Arrow 201 in trouble on landing. Observe main wheels, left side, turned out of position.

Arrow 201 crash sequence.

Aircraft swinging to left — drag chute attached.

Arrow starting to leave runway
— drag chute has been dropped.

Main gear collapsed — aircraft settling.

Arrow comes to rest — fully on ground.

Skid marks on runway show path of aircraft during landing run — Arrow can be seen in distance.

To Jan Zurakowski it was just another part of the flight test program and showed up a need for further modification in this area. The necessary modifications were made and the program continued on.

On August 1st, the second Arrow became airborne. This flight lasted about one hour and thirty-five minutes, the purpose being primarily to assess the aircraft's handling qualities at subsonic speeds.

Late on the afternoon of August 23rd, the aircraft was taken up for its second flight and contrails could be seen stretching across the skies from Georgian Bay to Lake Erie as the aircraft was flown at supersonic speeds for the first time.

Two successful flights were also made on August 26th each of approximately one hour duration, with #202 attaining speeds of Mach 1.62 and Mach 1.7 repectively.

On August 27th, Zura flew #202 around the Ottawa area for telemetry checks at speed up to Mach 1.5.

On Thursday August 28th, Zura again flew this same aircraft to Ottawa, made one circuit of Uplands Airport and returned to base. This was yet another telemetry check for #202. Early that same day Spud Potocki had the Arrow up for A.F.C.S. handling tests. Speeds recorded were Mach 1.7 on the first flight and Mach 1.72 on the latter flight.

Arrow #202 was standing by on the 6th of September, ready to make a scheduled appearance at the Canadian National Exhibition Air Show, but unfortunately the show was cancelled due to adverse weather conditions.

Two flights were made by #202 on Sunday, September 14th. The flight undertaken during the afternoon included turns in flight at supersonic speeds. Both flights also included checking of the A.F.C.S. handling. During the afternoon flight, Zura took Arrow 202 to Mach 1.86 at 50,500 feet. This was the highest speed attained by Zura prior to his retirement from test flying.

The primary purpose of the flight made on Tuesday, September 16th, was to investigate buffeting effects, and Dutch roll, as well as further A.F.C.S. checks. Zura sustained 2.2G's at Mach 1.2 on this flight.

The third Arrow #203 had reached the stage where taxi-tests were being carried out. The first taxi test, during which A.F.C.S. checks were made, took place on September 9th.

On September 22nd, the first flight of the third prototype took place and on this, its very first flight, exceeded the speed of sound, sustaining a speed of Mach 1.2.

September 26th saw #202 flying twice in one day. The first flight was subsonic to check the pitch damper, while in the later flight, Zura took the Arrow up to Mach 1.55

Single Engine Testing

Single engine flying with the J-75 engine was good, but depended on the weight of the aircraft, and the configuration that the aircraft was in at the time of simulated failure. On landing, the air brake was lowered on the Arrow, and then the gear. The aircraft drag would increase and it needed a fair amount of thrust in order to keep it level. When one engine was off for a single engine approach and landing, it could be carried out without the use of the afterburner. However, the afterburner could be used at times to allow for an error in judgement on the approach. It was possible to push the afterburner on and off without any swing to the aircraft at all. All the aircraft felt, was the great increase in power, possibly 5,000 to 6,000 lbs. extra thrust. (Any normal aircraft under this condition would register a swing which of course would be very dangerous near the ground.) This ability, to accept extra thrust and remain controllable, was one of the functions of the automatic flight control system being tested.

As the testing continued, the aircraft gradually grew more docile and manageable. For example, when the Arrow was first landed, touchdown speed was 185 knots. The aircraft felt right at this speed, but later the speed was lowered to 145 knots as the control system was improved. The Arrow was once landed, using less than 3,000 feet of runway.

On September 28th, Jack Woodman flew to assess the handling of the Arrow for the RCAF, at speeds up to Mach 1.7. Later that same day Spud carried out tests with speeds up to Mach 1.55. During this flight, Spud sustained 3G's at Mach 1.3 at 36,000 ft. These were the 13th and 14th flights of Arrow 202.

The Manager of the flight test department of Avro was Don Rogers, who had long been associated with test flying at the Malton complex. Don had been a pilot instructor at Hamilton, Ontario during WW2; test pilot on Lancaster bombers built at Victory Aircraft, Malton; Chief test pilot on the Avro Jetliner and CF-100 programs.

Zura signs and accepts Arrow 202 for its maiden flight.

At about the time of the 14th flight of #202 Jan Zurakowski retired from active test flying of the Arrows. Zura was still very involved with the program, but in an advisory capacity. It was fortunate that Avro had the services of such an experienced pilot.

Spud Potocki took over as Chief Experimental test pilot, from this point, and together with Peter Cope, were the only two Avro pilots flying Arrows. The RCAF pilot Jack Woodman had completed 2 hours and 5 minutes flying on the Arrow and his fellow pilot RCAF, F/Lt. Norm Ronaason, was prepared for his first flight on the aircraft. Norm had carried out cockpit familiarization and had completed his taxi test trials. It is reported that Norm actually taxied one of the Arrows out for his first flight, the day before cancellation, but due to some minor snag on the aircraft, decided not to take a chance on flying it.

He did not get another opportunity.

On October 1st Spud took up the Arrow 203 for its second flight and a speed of Mach 1.7 was reached.

October 3rd saw Spud flying Arrow 202 investigating pitch oscillation.

On the same day, another pilot, Peter Cope, joined the team of Arrow pilots, making his first flight in Arrow 202. This was mainly a familiarization flight which lasted 65 minutes with the Arrow flying at speeds up to Mach 1.5 at altitudes up to 49,000 — 50,000 feet.

We asked Peter Cope if he could remember any of his Arrow flights. He told us that, as he only flew the Arrow five times, three of these were interesting enough to remember.

"By way of elaboration, there was a hydraulic failure on my third flight (October 31st, Arrow 203) just at gear retraction, one of the nose gear

Arrow 202 meets two visiting Vulcan bombers at Malton. The Vulcans had flown across the Atlantic to participate in the Canadian International Air Show at Toronto (1958).

#202 in steep turn.

Classic view of Arrow 202 in flight.

Fueling up prior to flight test.

Gear down flight testing to check handling characteristics.

#202 on approach to Runway #14 Malton passing Village of Malton;
Orenda Engine Plant seen above aircraft.

Arrow 202 with air brakes extended flies over Malton (Toronto) Airport.

F86 Sabre chase plane comes in close for Arrow inspection on low speed testing
(Sabre dive brakes lowered).

hydraulic lines ruptured at a flareless fitting. Jack Woodman flying chase plane spotted the hydraulic fluid pouring out and advised me to select gear down, before all the hydraulic fluid was lost. The rest of the flight was taken up in some low speed gear down work until the weight (fuel) was reduced suitably for landing."

"On my 4th flight, November 7th, I had the air conditioning run wild. The system would only pump out cold air complete with ice and snow pellets; nothing I tried would shut the wretched unit off. I recall I was so damned cold when I landed that I had to be helped out of the cockpit. My teeth were literally chattering and it was 20 minutes or so before my legs felt as though they still belonged to me." One must remember that the Arrow's air conditioning system was capable of producing 23 tons of ice per day.

Peter Cope's final flight, in Arrow 204, resulted in an unscheduled landing at RCAF Station Trenton, February 2nd, 1959.

"I can recall the landing at Trenton; this was the only Arrow flight that landed away from base, and was brought about by a Viscount which elected to retract its landing gear right at the intersection of the two main runways at Malton. The remaining runway was considered too short for an Arrow landing at that time. I recall the Trenton landing was of interest, as my previous landing on the airplane had been without the services of my drag chute, (it failed to open). Consequently I made the slowest approach that I had made up till that time; however, my drag chute worked splendidly and I came to a stop, about half way along the 8,000 foot runway."

The flight test program was moving along at a fairly rapid pace, various problems were being encountered, general things you would expect to happen with an aircraft as complex as the Arrow; however, none of these problems was insurmountable. One must remember that problems are normally associated with the development of any new aircraft, and with the Arrow taking such a gigantic step forward, some of the problems tended to be magnified and more complex.

Spud Potocki flew Arrow 201 on October 5th, the first time since its accident. The flight was subsonic. Spud also flew Arrow 202 the same day on its 17th flight using all dampers up to Mach 1.45

On October 6th Peter Cope took Arrow 203 up for performance tests on the 1 A tailcones at speeds up to Mach 1.7 at 50,000 feet.

Fuel consumption and level speed checks at 35,000 feet at subsonic speeds were carried out on October 16th by Spud Potocki in Arrow 203.

Arrow 203 had undercarriage door trouble on the starboard side on its flight on October 17th so a low speed, gear down flight prevailed.

On October 18th, the weather was perfect; Arrow 203 took off on runway #32, unstick was a bit fast, 170 knots, with the nose gear coming off around 140 knots. On unstick the side slip indicator showed several degrees of port side slip for balanced flight; there was not much interference from lack of the A.F.C.S. on take off.

Gear up was not selected until the Sabre chase plane joined the Arrow to visually check gear retractions. While climbing to 25,000 feet, the Arrow went supersonic and then the aircraft stabilized at test Mach numbers.

A red light at Mach 0.95 aborted Woodman's hope for a high speed run in #203 on October 19th.

The pilot complained that the use of amber warning lights was useless in direct sunlight and that they had to be covered with both hands to see if any lights were coming on or not, also the new experimental control panel was badly placed and needed to be moved forward.

On October 27th, #204 took off for the first time. Take-off was normal with the A.F.C.S. off. Once airborne, however, the undercarriage on the starboard side was showing "unsafe" although the chase plane pilot confirmed that the wheels were properly retracted. The undercarriage was then lowered but the unsafe indication prevailed. Spud flew the aircraft with the undercarriage down for the rest of the flight while various tests were carried out.

Arrow 202 was also flying on October 27th and Spud flew Mach 1.5 at 42,000 feet while undergoing A.F.C.S. checks.

Two flights occurred on October 29th with #202, the first at Mach 1.7 the other at Mach 1.8 while Spud carried out flutter checks.

The flight on November 8th in #202 was subsonic as Spud carried out an assessment on the new modified elevator.

Second Accident, November 11th, 1958 (Program Flight #44)

The second accident happened on aircraft #202 flown by Spud Potocki. During a landing run, all four wheels skidded and the tires burst. The pilot lost directional control and the aircraft ran off the runway, damaging the right undercarriage leg.

The initial impression was that it was pilot

Flight line showing Arrows 201, 202 and 204.

Trouble in the automatic flight control system resulted in difficulties on landing, leading to brake lock up as witnessed in these dramatic photographs.

Spud Potok in total disbelief!

Spud walking down wing after crash (photo autographed by Spud).

View of the crash as seen from the front of aircraft.

error; the pilot applying too much braking pressure too early and locking the wheels.

The telemetry system recording basic parameters of flight, recorded that during touchdown the elevators suddenly moved full 30° down. Spud was sure that he did not move the controls and instrumentation experts suspected an error in recordings.

Fortunately, three young aviation enthusiasts were illegally on the airfield at the time, and took photographs of both the landing and the resultant crash. Avro were most happy to process these films immediately, as no company photographer had recorded this particular landing. After prints were made, it was clear that the elevators had in fact been fully down. Elevators on the Arrow were large, as is usual on delta designed aircraft.

It was unfortunate that this trouble resulted in an accident on landing, but most fortunate that it did not happen in flight, as a movement of 30° down on the elevator at anything above 200 to 300 knots, could have resulted in the complete disintegration of the aircraft within seconds and probably the loss of a valuable Test Pilot.

Recollections of Spud Potocki on Flight #44

Memories of this flight and the subsequent landing problems with Arrow 202, on November 11th, 1958, were fresh in Spud's mind when interviewed.

..."I was coming in to land after the flight and on the approach, I could feel my elevators getting very spongy, there was an excessive tendency to nose over on the airplane. This quickly cleared itself and I didn't worry about it, although I believe I called the air traffic control, to tell them I had a bit of a problem in the control circuit. I had crossed the airfield boundary by this time and it seemed to be quite a normal landing. It was rather fast, but quite normal. I may have landed a little fast due to gusty wind conditions, at the time.

After I touched down on the main gear and lowered the nose of the aircraft to the ground, I detected essentially that the aircraft did not seem to have any brakes. Normally it was my habit on all aircraft I ever flew, that after touchdown, I would just "peck" at the brakes to see that I was getting brake response; it would be far better to take off again and align yourself for a slower approach and landing, if there was any possibility of brake trouble.

Just like driving a car under these conditions

— you suddenly realize how fast you are going and push really hard on the brakes. I immediately thought of the possibility of trouble of some sort. As we now know, my brakes were fully on and locked. They stayed locked thereafter. As I recall I was rather short on fuel at that time and under these conditions, I would not have given much thought to going around again, because I am sure that the flight must have been one of the hardest on fuel carried out on any Arrow. I remember I took the aircraft up around Lake Superior in order to get a good stabilized run for my 1.98 Mach run. This run was from about Lake Superior to Ottawa. I mentioned Lake Superior and I am sure it was fairly close to there that the high speed run was started. I recall I had climbed to something like 50,000 feet to get cleared to the 1.98 Mach number.

At lower altitudes I was restricted to keep to lower Mach numbers. This particular flight was restricted to and terminated at Mach 1.98, which was mentioned in the local papers the next day, so it was no secret. Having used a lot of fuel, I gave little or no thought to going around again, I just made the best of conditions as they seemed to be and attempted to complete a normal landing. I opened the tail chute which did not seem to do much good. In the meantime my brakes were still locked and I suppose I kept them that way not knowing that they were already burning into the drums. What eventually happened was this. The heat generated by locked brakes burnt through the brake drums and the tires exploded. I lost control of the aircraft, which swung to the right and off the runway. The right main gear collapsed and I came to a grinding halt with my right wing tip dragging the ground.

I got out of the cockpit and walked down the right wing to the ground. I had a look at things, and at the time I was not really sure of just what had gone wrong. I was rather downfallen of what could have gone wrong with the aircraft. I was looking around the back of the aircraft when Zura arrived, with some other chaps. I had a talk with Zura, because he was of course the "Good old father of the Arrow", and probably knew more about the aircraft than anyone else; he said, "Spud, look at the position of your elevators." We looked and the elevators were 'down' some 20° or so. It was determined at the accident investigation that there was some trouble in the automatic control system to the elevator, which after I had lowered the aircraft nose onto the ground, drove my elevator to the fully down position. In doing

Additional crash view showing drag chute still attached.

Aircraft resting on right wing with main right hand gear totally collapsed.

this, it created lift on the aircraft which was landing fairly fast. As you probably know the Arrow had no flaps, and was what is known in the business, as a rather 'hot' plane. With full elevator down, there was generated what you might call 'back lift' on the aircraft, to give an apparent reduction of weight on the main gear wheels of about half of the total weight of the aircraft when brakes should have been applied. This is why my 'peck' on the brakes did not register as a braking effect. I had no way of knowing the elevator position in the cockpit as the control column would have been central with the nose wheel on the ground. A pilot does not play around with the elevator controls at that time."

Spud and the Arrow

We asked Spud if the accident was the most serious problem he had experienced while flying the Arrows?

"Yes I would think so. I had other minor problems as you would expect when test flying any new type. On a number of flights, there were burst tires on landing and times when the drag chute failed to operate as required, together with minor troubles in flight. There was one situation I remember that rather scared me, and I don't get scared very easily, while flying aircraft. It was found that I had about a 15 second break in my transmissions to the ground. I recall that this was while I was testing longitudinal damping; this involves heaving the aircraft up and down violently, accelerating it to something like 3G in pitch, then releasing the controls and seeing how they respond to this sort of input. I was climbing to around 25,000 feet in a fairly steep climb attitude, with the sun shining over my left shoulder onto the control panel. A nuisance light came on but did not seem serious; air conditioning trouble of some sort. I recall, I leaned forward onto my safety straps to turn the trouble light off, when suddenly the aircraft took off by itself, it gave me quite a rough ride; I had possibly 3 to 4G positive then 2 to 3G negative in a rapid oscillation motion with a frequency of one second or less, which is rather rapid. The aircraft did a sort of porpoise on its own, up-down, up-down several times.

There is not much a pilot can do when an aircraft starts flying on its own. This was the one case that such a thing happened and I demobilized the automatic flying control system instantly.

A strange thing about the Arrow, when it was on automatic flight control system, the stick was in neutral, and when the rapid oscillation occurred, I automatically gripped the stick and acted in opposition to this oscillation. In fact, I dampened the motion of the aircraft. Of course, all these wiggles went through the telemetry to the ground and the ground asked 'What the hell are you doing with the aircraft, Spud? We are getting some very peculiar signals here on the ground.' I said, "don't ask me. Tell me what is going on up here! I am doing nothing but the aircraft has a mind of its own."

This was the only condition in which I was worried in any of my flights in any of the Arrows. It was a situation in which I did nothing to the controls but something happened within the aircraft itself. It had a fluctuating response; some feedback from the structure into the control system and the aircraft started acting in a divergent manner on me. Luckily, I caught it quick enough and nothing serious happened. I returned to base immediately and the aircraft was thoroughly checked over. One thing! it was on the telemetry record and easily noted to be a very violent motion and not pilot generated, but system generated. It was something we at Avro worried a fair amount about, at the time, as we could find no reason."

Fly-By-Wire (A.F.C.S.)

We asked Spud Potocki to recall something about the fly-by-wire system....." "The Arrow as you probably know was an aircraft "flown by wire", in its final stages. I'm not sure that the average person would realize just how really advanced the Arrow was. In fact the only other aircraft I know of to "fly by wire" between the Avro Arrow and 1971 was the X 15 experimental, which was the North American Aviation stratospheric hypersonic aircraft. Some experiments had been carried out at Cornell University on "fly by wire" on the F-86 Sabre; one of the two seaters. We had the Arrow in 1958 flying on an electric signal. How was this done? The pilot had in the control column some form of feel spring, which when he put a half pound of pressure on the column an electric contact would close within the base of the column and send a signal to the control system via amplifiers and electronics to the control servos. This was an electronic hydraulic jack which in turn moved the control surfaces themselves. The pilot would get response to his small movement and pressure on the control column. If he increased pressure on the column, the electronics

#203 over Malton Airport. Note the rods of varying lengths on rear of fuselage near underside of tail cones. These were used to register cone clearance from the runway on landing.

Arrow's 203 (early day-glow) and 202 standing on flight line. Photo taken from wing of B-47 bomber.

would respond proportionally with rapid movements to the aircraft controls. Superimposed on top of this was a differential servo which was connected to the damping system that moved the controls completely independent of the pilot's control column in the cockpit.

The pilot could move the column in one direction while the control itself would possibly move in the opposite direction. This was part of the complexity of the 'Arrow fly-by-wire systems.'

When all the bugs were out of the Arrow, it would be a fully automatic aircraft with the pilot an emergency factor only. The pilot would start the engines, taxi the aircraft to the take-off point, and the plane would in effect be able to fly itself. The pilot would simply keep an eye on things and take over in an emergency. After its mission, the aircraft would be capable of landing itself with the pilot simply taxiing the aircraft back to park it. The reason — with interception at supersonic speeds, human reaction would be too slow. It would require fully automatic control from the ground to intercept something flying at 1,000 to 1,500 mph. Time is a great factor and manoeuverability at that kind of closing speed is very limited.

At Mach 2 which is around 1,300 mph the radius of turn is in the order of 15 miles so the problems are colossal.

The Arrow was to be fully automatic with everything done by black boxes. We call them computers today.

I recall many times while flying chase in the CF-100 on Jan Zurakowski, I would watch the Arrow control surfaces and the movements would not make sense to me. Remember, Jan would be telling me on radio what his control stick movements were. The system would be sensing and applying corrections to the aircraft without the pilot really being aware of it. For example, it was a completely synthetic control system.

Normally if a twin engined airplane loses one engine, by failure or by the pilot simulating failure, the aircraft would immediately create a sideslip and roll; on the Arrow, when it was in the fly-by-wire mode, the aircraft would remain steady. I recall flying the Arrow in something like an angle of 60 degrees climb with full afterburner cut in and I would chop one engine. It was amazing to watch the sideslip instrument remain perfectly steady when the automatic control system took over instantly to keep the aircraft steady and

Arrow 203 fuelling up as another Arrow passes overhead.

Aircraft shown in early day-glow markings while being serviced.
The Red Ensign has now been applied to tail, the only Arrow to have had such marking applied.

Arrow 203 being serviced during the winter. Later day-glow markings are now in evidence. Arrow 201
may be observed to the left wearing its day-glow paint.

Chute streaming behind Arrow 203 as it returns to parking area.

#203 being readied for next flight.

Arrow 203 crosses over Southern Ontario farm land with chase planes close at hand.

Upon landing, pilot Spud Potocki compares notes with observer, Red Darrah
(the only passenger ever to fly in an Arrow).

Ground crew congratulates flight crew on this historic occasion.

straight. Speed of course would fall off rapidly in such a steep climb.

A number of times I had carried out completely automatic takeoffs and landings, as well as taking the aircraft fully through its entire flight envelope. The Arrow "fly-by-wire" control system was easily the most advanced in the world in 1958."

Arrow to Pull 2 G's

First of all, almost any airplane can pull 2 G's, even a modern civil airplane has no problem pulling 2 G's. You can get 2 G's in turbulence very easily. The real trick is to be able to pull that G without a loss in speed or altitude.

The Arrow's specification stated that the aircraft must be able to manoeuver at a rate of 2G, at an altitude of 50,000 feet and at a speed of Mach 1.5 without any loss of speed or altitude. This is a very stringent requirement indeed and dictates the structural strength of the aircraft, together with the excess power that must be available from the engine at this high altitude.

This was achieved with the Arrow using the J-75 engines at about 50,000 feet. The company

felt that they could meet this specification at 60,000 feet with the Iroquois engines in the Arrow.

The reason for this optimism by the company was due to the extra thrust that would be available from the Iroquois at this higher altitude compared to the J-75 engines.

Red Darrah the Arrow's Only Passenger

The Arrow only carried a passenger on one occasion. It was D.E. (Red) Darrah flying in Arrow 203, piloted by Spud Potocki, on February 19th. Red was in the rear cockpit essentially fine tuning the 'fly-by-wire' system for Spud.

Spud would ask Red to set up a certain condition on the system to give more or less damping to pitch, roll or yaw. Spud would then check the systems operation to ensure that he was getting the best response possible. Spud reports that "things went very well, Red was doing a fine job of tuning and calibrating, but unfortunately we only had one flight together." The following day the entire project was cancelled!

Arrow 203 as seen with airbrakes extended.

Arrow 204 was airborne for only 65 minutes, November 22nd, as Spud carried out a simple check flight.

On November 30th Spud flew Arrow 204 on its third flight for a configuration of snag clearance to Mach 1.2.

Spud's flight on December 11th, in Arrow 201, was to check the closing of the undercarriage doors, while the gear was in the down position. The new modified elevator controls were also checked.

On December 15th, Arrow 201's speed was restricted due to a gear unsafe indication thus limiting the flight to damper system checks.

On the 20th of December, #201 took off on a flight, intended to probe into the high 'G' region at speeds up to 550 knots; however, on retracting the undercarriage the starboard door failed to lock up. The chase aircraft indicated there was a gap of between 3/8 and ½" at the door. After four or five extensions the conditions remained the same, so the high 'G' work had to be abandoned. Modifications were carried out to the door mechanism and the aircraft flew again the next day; unfortunately the same thing happened.

Next day Dowty's were brought in, (the manufacturers of the landing gear), and after dismantling the leg it was found that a locking clip had become displaced and jammed. It was considered too risky to fly any aircraft with Mark 1 undercarriage since they all had this type of locking clip. Avro was left with the situation where the only undercarriage that could be cleared for flight was on aircraft #205, since it had Mark 1A gear that included modification in this area. The preflight department was unhappy about having to give up #205's undercarriage as it was hoped to fly Arrow 205 by the end of the year. Since there were problems with #205's starboard engine due to oil traces in the exhaust pipe, the gear was exchanged between #205 and #201. This allowed #205 to continue engine running and taxiing tests.

Spud took up #201 again on January 5th to record two flights for the day; the first dealt with damper system checks to 20,000 feet, the second flight being an extension of the first.

Arrow 205 continued to have oil warning light problems during preflight testing. Finally everything appeared okay, and the aircraft was cleared for first flight. It took off for the first time on January 11th, 1959, and shortly into the flight

#204 undergoing servicing with aircraft painted in intermediate day-glow
(day-glow has now been added to nose section).

Arrow 204 taxis out for a winter flight, snow is quite evident.

Arrow 204 in flight.

Landing with airbrakes extended, after another successful flight test.

The end of an era was marked at Avro when a short informal ceremony took place as the last (692nd) CF-100 rolled out of Bay #3 — on schedule to the very day planned four years earlier. Arrow 204 now shows full day-glow (fin & rudder).

program Spud got an oil warning light and decided to shut the engine down to avoid possible damage. He managed to get the aircraft safely back to Malton on one engine, after a pretty traumatic flight lasting only 40 minutes. The engine was then removed as no one could figure out how oil was getting through the system. Upon dismantling the engine it was discovered that a seal in the gear box had leaked back through the engine. Partly because of this problem #205 never flew again before cancellation.

Arrow 201 continued damper system checks and the elevator hinge movement tests on January 17th, on a flight lasting approximately 1 hour.

Arrow 203's 10th flight on January 20th was a check flight to Mach 1.7 with a modified elevator system.

On January 24th Jack Woodman in #201 carried out damper system checks. Jack, who hadn't flown an Arrow since October, reported that the general handling characteristics had improved since his last flight. This flight was restricted to low levels only, due to weather.

Spud continued general damper handling tests on #201 on its next flight on January 27th.

Spud flew #201 on two short flights on January 31st, to do an extension of the flight envelope.

Jack Woodman's last flight was in #203 on February 1st. He reported that both longitudinal and lateral controls were good and the erratic control problems he had encountered on his previous flight in #203 had disappeared, also that at no time in the flight was there more than 1 degree of sideslip.

On February 2nd a flight of #204 diverted to Trenton as mentioned previously.

On February 3rd, #204 flown by Spud was ferried back to Malton with gear down.

Spud, flying #201 on February 7th, attained speeds up to Mach 1.3 while testing roll and sideslip.

Spud also flew #204 on February 7th (its last flight) but was limited to Mach 1.5 because of control pedal judder.

On the morning of February 19th, Spud and Red took up #203 for an hour and ten minutes. Later that afternoon Spud took up #201 for a short flight, reaching a speed of Mach 1.7; (little did he know at that time, it would be his last flight in an Arrow).

Friday, February 20th, 1959, will always be known to "AVROITES" as 'BLACK FRIDAY', for on that day the ARROW and IROQUOIS ENGINE died!

Arrow 204 take off
— with aircraft painted in
early day-glow.

Flight testing of airbrakes
with day-glow markings
on wingtips and rudder.

At altitude with vapour trail
created by leading edge notch
(day-glow has not yet been
applied to nose section).

Spud climbs aboard #204 for a check flight.

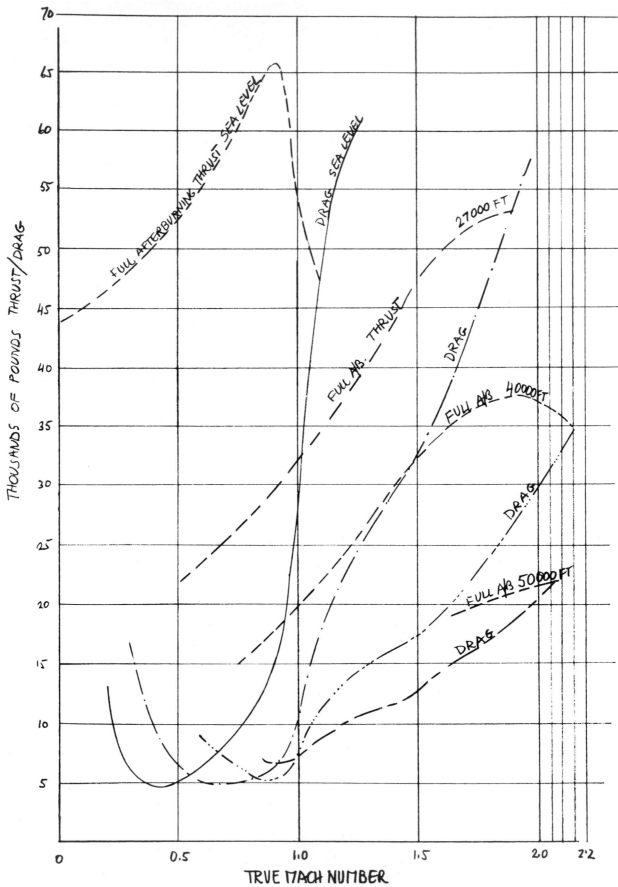

THOUSANDS OF POUNDS THRUST/DRAG

TRUE MACH NUMBER

AVRO ARROW MK I THRUST/DRAG RELATIONSHIP

GRAPH AS DRAWN BY TEST PILOT.

Pressure fueling of the Arrow.

Ground testing of the Arrow's air-conditioning system.

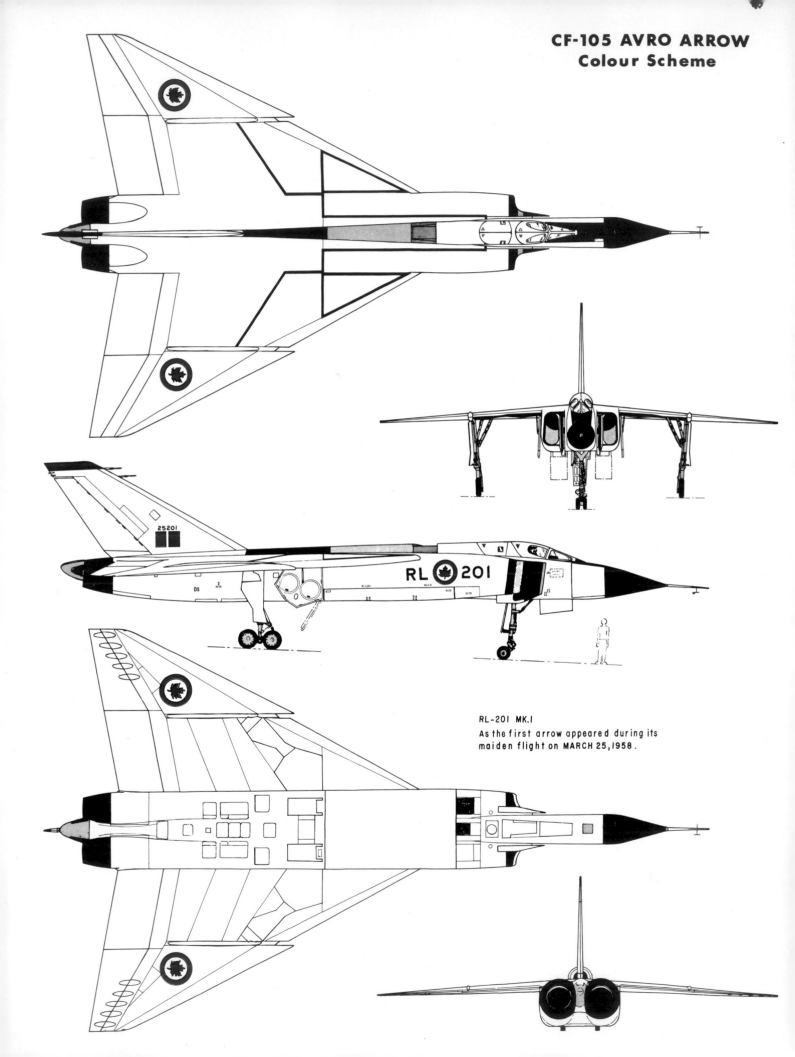

CF-105 AVRO ARROW
Colour Scheme

25201

RL 201

RL-201 MK.I
As the first arrow appeared during its
maiden flight on MARCH 25,1958.

1	U/C UP MODE - DAMPER TEST Switch	52	ENG BLEED Air Conditioning Warning Lights
2	IFF Control Panel	53	ENG BLEED AIR LH OFF-NORMAL - RH OFF Switch
3	DAMPING SYSTEM Circuit Breaker Panel	54	Map Light
4	DAMPER, POWER ON-OFF Switch	55	OXYGEN Quantity Gauge
5	DAMPER, EMERGENCY Push Button Switch	56	Console Flood Lights (2)
6	DAMPER, ENGAGE Push Button Switch	57	RAM AIR TURBINE Switch
7	Control Surface Response Indicator	58	NAV LIGHTS, FLASH-OFF-STEADY Switch
8	COMM. Radio Control Panel - ARC-34	59	ALTERNATORS RESET ON-OFF LH and RH Switches
9	High Altitude Flood Light	60	DC RESET Push Button
10	Console Flood Light	61	Console Light
11	RUDDER TRIM, LEFT-RIGHT Switch	62	COCKPIT LIGHTING Panel
12	FIRE Extinguisher SECOND SHOT Switch	63	HIGH ALT LIGHTING ON-OFF Switch
13	FIRE-Combined Warning Lights and Selector Switches, LH, HYD, RH	64	MAIN PANEL OFF-BRIGHT Selector
14	NAV BAIL OUT Warning Switch	65	CONSOLE PANELS OFF-BRIGHT Selector
15	L.P. FUEL COCKS Switches and Guards	66	CONSOLE FLOOD OFF-BRIGHT Selector
16	CROSSFEED, LH ONLY - NORMAL - RH ONLY Switch	67	AIR COND Panel
17	ENGINE FUEL, EMERG-RESET Switches and Guards	68	RAIN REPELLENT ON-OFF Switch (TEMP CONTROL/EMERG OFF. First aircraft).
18	Parachute Brake, STREAM - JETTISON Selector Lever	69	CABIN PRESS DUMP Switch
19	Throttle Levers, LH and RH	70	AIR SUPPLY NORM-OFF EMERG Switch
20	Console Flood Light	71	DEFOG ON-OFF Switch
21	SPEED BRAKE, IN-OUT Switch	72	TEMP COOL-WARM Selector
22	ANTI-SKID, NORM-EMERG-OFF Switch	73	Anti-g Valve Manual Override Button
23	LIGHTS LAND-TAXI-OFF Switch	74	INTER Control Panel
24	CANOPY CLOSE-OFF-OPEN Switch	75	UHF/IFF EMERG, PRESS TO TEST Button
25	ELEV TRIM DISENGAGE Switch	76	J4 COMP, AEROBATICS - NORMAL Switch
26	Landing Gear Control Lever, UP-DN	77	UHF ANT, UPPER-LOWER Switch
27	Landing Gear EMERGENCY EXTENSION Locking Latch Push-Button	78	RMI NEEDLE, TACAN-UHF HOMER Switch
28	Parking Brake Handle	79	RADIO COMPASS Panel
29	LANDING GEAR POSITION Indicator	80	J4 COMP - LAT Correction Controller
30	SKIN TEMP Indicator	81	J4 COMP - MAG/DG Selector Switch
31	Mach/Airspeed Indicator	82	J4 COMP - DECR/INCR/SET Switch
32	CHECK LIST, LANDING	83	J4 COMP - Hemisphere Selector Switch
33	Accelerometer	84	J4 COMP - Synchronizing Indicator (Annunciator)
34	Sideslip Indicator	85	ENGINE START, START-OFF-RESET, LH and RH Switches
35	Angle of Attack Indicator	86	MASTER ELEC ON-OFF Switch
36	NAV BAIL OUT Indicator	87	Warning Lights Panel
37	Red Master Warning Light	88	Rudder PEDAL ADJUST Handle
38	Amber Master Warning Light	89	RPM Indicators
39	Standby Magnetic Compass	90	Altimeter
40	RADIO MAGNETIC INDICATOR	91	Rudder Pedal Adjustment Label
41	FUEL QUANTITY Gauges	92	Turn and Slip Indicator
42	CHECK LIST TAKE OFF	93	Rate of Climb Indicator
43	Artificial Horizon Indicator	94	Automatic Mode Disengage Switch
44	GYRO ERECT Push Button	95	Elevator and Aileron Trim Button
45	EMERGENCY CANOPY OPENING Lever	96	Emergehcy Damping Engage Switch
46	Engine PRESSURE RATIO Gauges LH and RH	97	Nose Wheel Steering Selector
47	EXH TEMP Gauges LH and RH	98	Press-to-transmit Push Button
48	CABIN PRESSURE ALTITUDE Gauge	99	Throttles Friction Damper
49	PRESS TO RESET Push Button	100	Engine Relight Switch, LH and RH
50	DAY - NIGHT Switch		
51	PRESS TO TEST Switch		

A REPRESENTATIVE COLOUR SCHEME IS SHOWN
FOR EACH OF THE ARROWS DISPLAYED BETWEEN
OCTOBER 4,1957 (ROLL-OUT DATE) AND FEBRUARY 20,
1959 (CANCELLATION DATE).

Dayglo patches were changed frequently
because although primarily intended to
to show up an aircraft down on the snow,
exterior surfaces of the arrow under test
were painted dayglo to assist observers
to focus in on the component during
the flight test program.

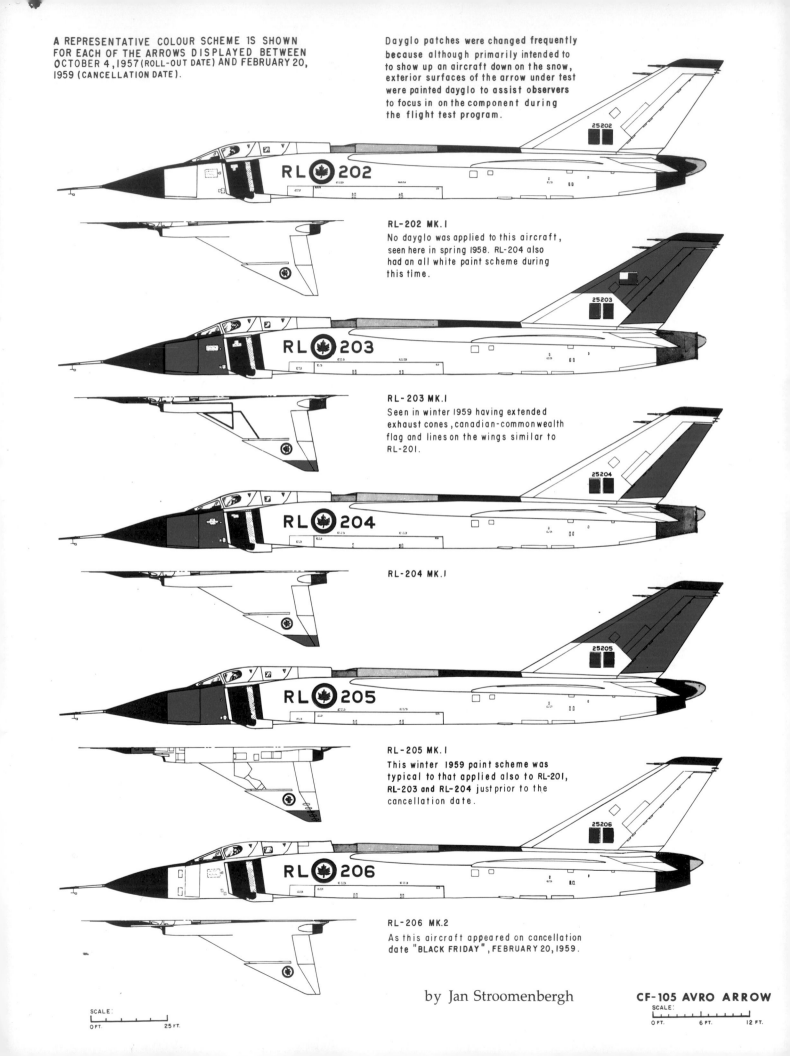

RL-202 MK.I
No dayglo was applied to this aircraft,
seen here in spring 1958. RL-204 also
had an all white paint scheme during
this time.

RL-203 MK.I
Seen in winter 1959 having extended
exhaust cones, canadian-commonwealth
flag and lines on the wings similar to
RL-201.

RL-204 MK.I

RL-205 MK.I
This winter 1959 paint scheme was
typical to that applied also to RL-201,
RL-203 and RL-204 just prior to the
cancellation date.

RL-206 MK.2
As this aircraft appeared on cancellation
date "BLACK FRIDAY", FEBRUARY 20, 1959.

by Jan Stroomenbergh

CF-105 AVRO ARROW

SCALE:
0 FT.   25 FT.

SCALE:
0 FT.   6 FT.   12 FT.

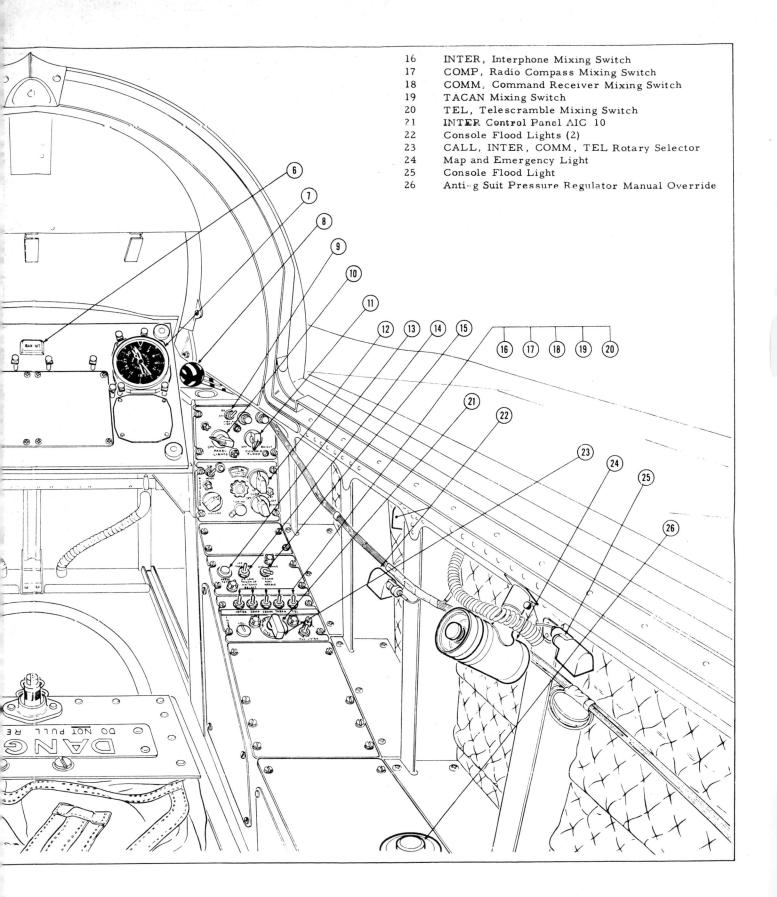

16 INTER, Interphone Mixing Switch
17 COMP, Radio Compass Mixing Switch
18 COMM, Command Receiver Mixing Switch
19 TACAN Mixing Switch
20 TEL, Telescramble Mixing Switch
21 INTER Control Panel AIC 10
22 Console Flood Lights (2)
23 CALL, INTER, COMM, TEL Rotary Selector
24 Map and Emergency Light
25 Console Flood Light
26 Anti-g Suit Pressure Regulator Manual Override

VER'S COCKPIT

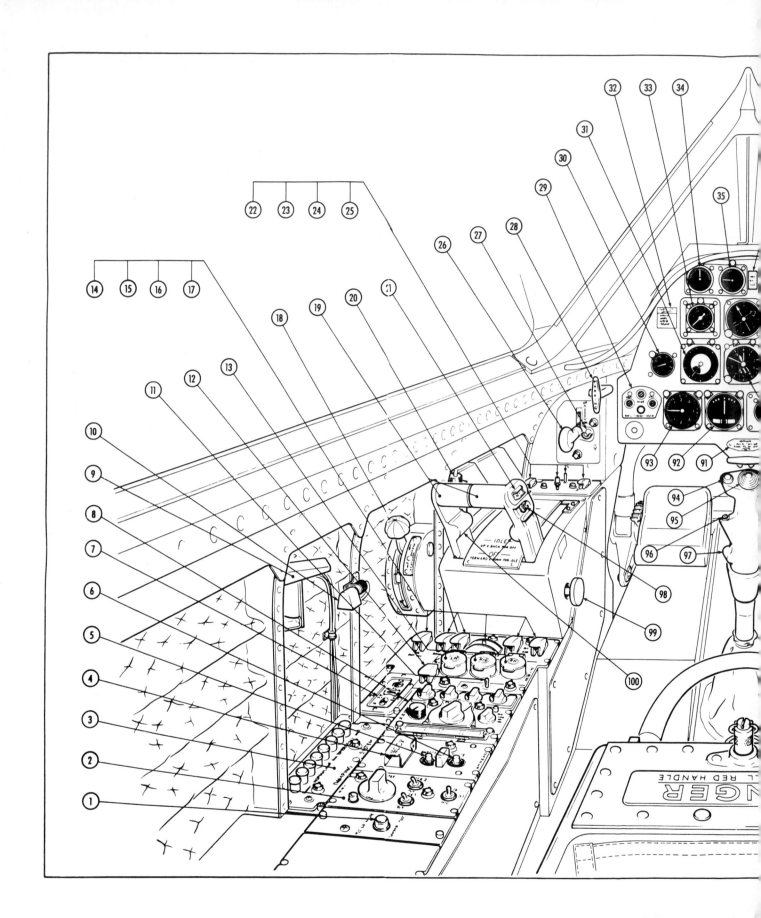

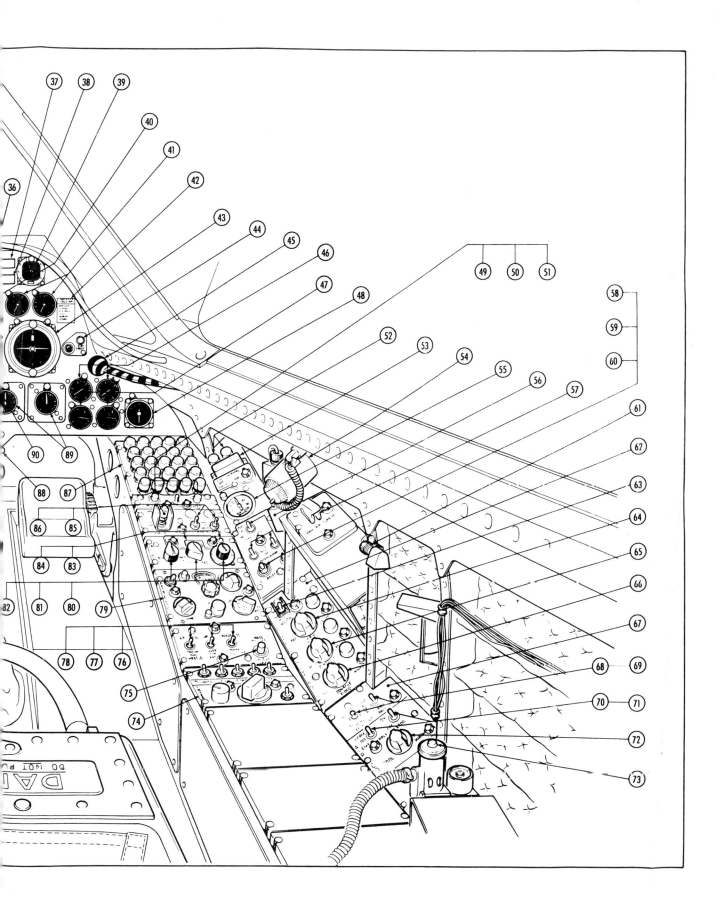

CKPIT

1   Console Flood Lights (3)
2   CANOPY, OPEN-OFF-CLOSE Switch
3   OXYGEN Quantity Gauge
4   Altimeter
5   Access Panel to Navigator's Canopy Locking Handle from
       Front Cockpit
6   Navigator's BAIL OUT Warning Light
7   RADIO MAGNETIC INDICATOR
8   EMERGENCY CANOPY OPENING Lever
9   HIGH ALT LIGHTING, ON-OFF Switch (Non-operative)
10   PANEL LIGHTS OFF-BRIGHT Selector Switch
11   CONSOLE FLOOD OFF-BRIGHT Selector Switch
12   RADIO COMPASS Control Panel ARN-6
13   PRESS TO TALK Switch
14   IFF-TACAN ANTENNA SELECT Switch
15   UHF HOMER - TACAN RMI NEEDLE Selector

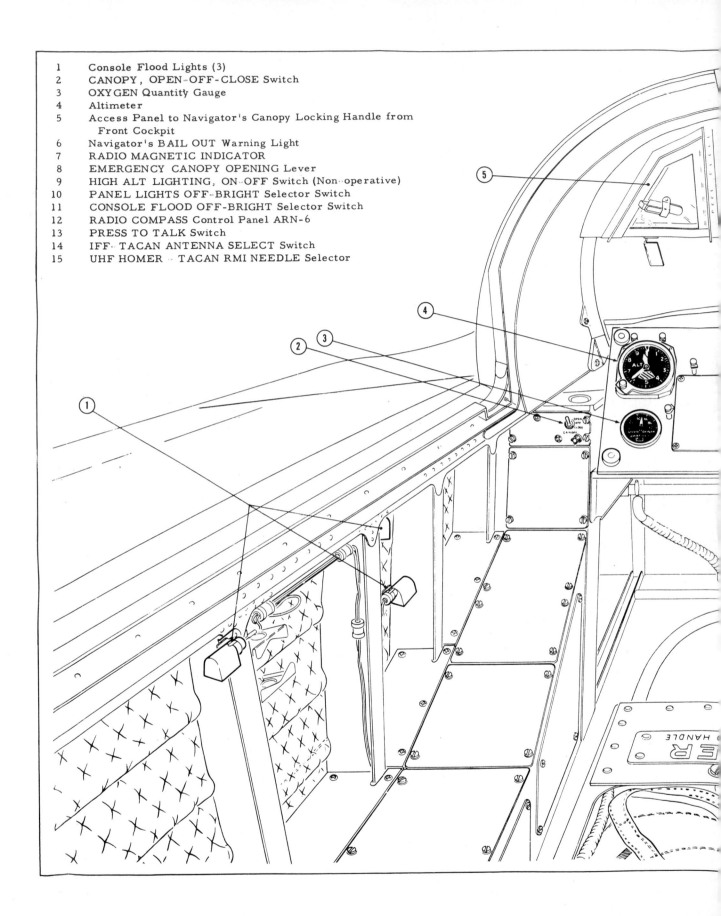

OBSER

Arrow 205 in hangar being prepared for first flight. Observe weapons pack dolly.

Arrow taxiing out for first flight.

#205's first and only take off.

Arrow 205 in for only landing.

(from movie film)

Landing run, full chute deployed.

Arrow 205 taxis back after its one and only short flight.

Roundels Distorted After High Speed Flight

It was reported after high speed flights of the Arrow that the roundels or circular Canadian maple leaf emblems on the side of the aircraft were distorted. This was true but not just because of temperature. There is a phenomenon that occurs at very high speed called "intake buzz". This is the interaction of the airflow over the engine intakes. This is very difficult to test on the ground because the interaction only takes place in flight.

The Arrow experienced "buzz" and this caused a buckling of the outer fuselage skin covering the area of the intakes, thus causing the roundels and identification numbers to distort. This problem was corrected simply by the use of thicker fuselage skin covering.

#201 taxiing out to last flight.

'ON FINAL' Feb. 19th, 1959 (approx. 14.20 hrs.) Arrow 201 on its final approach.
This was to become the last flight of an Arrow in the Arrow Project. (from movie film)

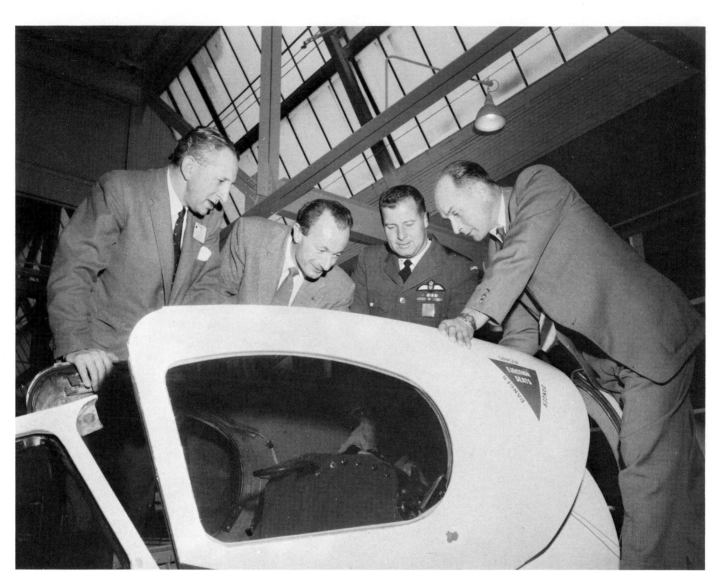

The only four test pilots to fly the Arrow (L-R) Company Pilots Spud Potocki, Peter Cope; R.C.A.F. Test Pilot F/Lt. Jack Woodman, and Chief Test Pilot Jan Zurakowski.

Jack F. Woodman

5

The Log Book

We are indeed fortunate that a complete copy of the Flight Times of all the Arrows has survived and has been made available.

Tables and remarks in this Chapter are therefore provided from the official Avro flight office records.

Luckily we have also been able to confirm the accuracy of all this information by inspection of a handwritten record kept by Test Pilot 'Spud' Potocki during the program, and made available by Don Rogers.

We have had at our disposal copies of the President, and General Manager's report to the Avro Board of Directors and it is difficult to understand why his staff listed Flight Times in these reports that are at variance with those of the Avro Flight Office.

The official Avro flight office record contains, with one exception, the actual take off and landing times of all flights. In doing so it provides some very interesting facts and clears up several debatable questions that have persisted over the intervening years. Previous to this official record being made available, photo copies of the pilot's log books all showed minor discrepancies. This is not surprising since many pilots record their time differently! For example, do you include time for taxiing out, and back from the actual take-off and landing? Another factor became obvious from a conversation with Jan Zurakowski; "I may well have flown the Arrow more than is recorded in my log book. It was a busy time with the project moving at a hectic pace. It seemed unimportant at

the time to keep close record on such things as personal flight times."

One of the most persistent remarks heard during research, was "two Arrows seen flying in formation." This can be dispelled quite easily upon inspection of the Chronological Flight Log. The first possible double flight is noted for April 18th, 1958 (2 flights), but obviously the same pilot could not fly the same aircraft in formation with himself. The same is true of August 26th, 1958, another would be August 28th, 1958, different pilots but the same aircraft. Yet another possible would be October 5th, 1958, different aircraft, but at the same time, same pilot. As again, on October 27th, 1958, February 7th, 1959, and on February 19th, 1959. It has been confirmed that there were, in fact, plans to get two Arrows up together on several occasions, but due to minor unserviceability or other factors it did not take place. One such plan was for the 1958 Canadian National Exhibition Air Show. Since an Arrow photo was used on the CNE AIR SHOW program, it was hoped to fly at least one Arrow (possibly two) in formation with a R.A.F. Avro Vulcan "delta" bomber which had flown from Farnborough, England, for the show. A quick check of the Chronological Log shows that no Arrow was flown on the Air Show dates. Plans had also been discussed to have two Arrows fly over Uplands Airport in Ottawa, during October 1958, when squadrons of the RCAF with CF-100's departed for Europe. This was not done as it was considered too risky to fly two valuable aircraft when it was

Arrow over Niagara Falls.

only possible to have one aircraft on telemetry at one time. It should be pointed out to the reader, that a photo showing two Arrows in formation and widely distributed during the Arrow program, was actually the work of an Avro Aircraft artist, as well as a fake painting of two Arrows in formation, shown on the September 1958 Reader's Digest cover. Another reputedly fake photo often seen, is a beautiful picture showing RL 25201 perfectly centered over Niagara Falls.

Other interesting facts that can be obtained from the tables include: Aircraft #201 had the highest flying time of 25 hours 40 minutes, even though it experienced undercarriage trouble on landing June 11th, 1958, and did not fly again until October 5th, 1958. On November 11th, 1958, Aircraft #202 also had trouble on landing (flying controls that developed into undercarriage trouble). Because of its repair and modification it did not fly again prior to the cancellation of the program. Aircraft #203 was the last aircraft test flown by Jan Zurakowski prior to his retirement from a very distinguished test flying career. Together with #202 it was the only other Arrow flown by all four test pilots. Arrow 203 was the only Arrow to carry an official passenger (Red

Darrah). This flight was carried out on February 19th, 1959, the day prior to cancellation. Red was in the rear cockpit, tuning the fly-by-wire system for the pilot, Spud Potocki. Aircraft #204 was the only Arrow to land away from home base, on February 2nd, 1959. This was not due to trouble with the Arrow but was caused by a minor landing accident to a Trans Canada (now Air Canada) airliner, which was obstructing the main landing runway at Malton. The Arrow diversion was most appropriately to the Royal Canadian Air Force Base at Trenton, Ontario. It was known that the Arrow was taken to Trenton by Peter Cope, but he had no record in his log book of the return flight. Spud Potocki on the other hand had no record in his log book of having returned the aircraft to Malton and did not remember doing so. It was speculated for a while that this could be the "Phantom Arrow" that had been rumoured to have survived the cancellation cut up. Sad to say, the Avro flight office records set the record straight and showed that Potocki had in fact returned the aircraft to Malton on February 3rd, 1959. #205 had the saddest history of all the Arrows — a short 40 minutes maiden flight and then cut up, by Avro welders.

#204 at Trenton; the only Arrow to have landed away from home base. The Bay of Quinte, Ontario, can be seen in the background.

CHRONOLOGICAL FLIGHT LOG OF THE AVRO ARROW

Flight Test No.	Date (1958)	Aircraft No.	Pilot	Time of Lift-off & Touchdown	Max. Speed Flown in Mach #	Flight Duration Hrs/Min	Aircraft Flight
1	March 25	25201	Zura	9:51 10:26		0 35	1
2	April 1	25201	Zura	18:15 19:05	0.65	0 50	2
3	April 3	25201	Zura	10:00 11:05	1.1	1 05	3
4	April 15	25201	Zura	15:15 16:30		1 15	4
5	April 17	25201	Zura	11:25 12:35		1 10	5
6	April 18	25201	Zura	13:35 14:30	1.25	0 55	6
7	April 18	25201	Zura	16:40 17:20	1.52	0 40	7
8	April 22	25201	Woodman	16:30 17:40	1.4	1 10	8
9	April 23	25201	Potocki	15:10 15:55	1.2	0 45	9
10	June 7	25201	Zura	14:30 16:15		1 45	10
11	June 11	25201	Zura	14:10 15:30	0.9	1 20	11*
			*Suffered Landing accident				
12	Aug 1	25202	Zura	14:45 16:20		1 35	1
13	Aug 23	25202	Zura	17:35 18:35	1.5	1 00	2
14	Aug 26	25202	Zura	11:05 12:10	1.62	1 05	3
15	Aug 26	25202	Zura	15:30 16:30	1.7	1 00	4
16	Aug 27	25202	Zura	16:20 17:25	1.5	1 05	5
17	Aug 28	25202	Potocki	10:45 11:50	1.7	1 05	6
18	Aug 28	25202	Zura	15:50 17:10	1.72	1 20	7

Flight Test No.	Date (1958)	Aircraft No.	Pilot	Time of Lift-off & Touchdown	Max. Speed Flown in Mach #	Flight Duration Hrs/Min		Aircraft Flight
19	Sept 14	25202	Zura	10:40 11:45		1	05	8
20[1]	Sept 14	25202	Zura	16:35 17:45	1.89	1	10	9
21	Sept 16	25202	Zura	15:05 16:15	1.2	1	10	10
22	Sept 22	25203	Zura	13:40 15:15	1.2	1	35	1
23	Sept 26	25202	Zura	11:50 12:55		1	05	11
24	Sept 26	25202	Zura	18:10 19:10	1.55	1	00	12
25	Sept 28	25202	Woodman	10:45 11:40	1.7	0	55	13
26	Sept 28	25202	Potocki	16:50 17:35	1.55	0	45	14
27	Oct 1	25203	Potocki	13:50 14:35	1.7	0	45	2
28	Oct 3	25202	Potocki	11:55 13:20		1	25	15
29	Oct 3	25202	Cope	16:15 17:20	1.5	1	05	16
30	Oct 5	25201	Potocki	10:35 11:55		1	20	12
31	Oct 5	25202	Potocki	16:50 17:40	1.45	0	50	17
32	Oct 6	25203	Cope	10:40 11:40	1.7	1	00	3
33	Oct 16	25203	Potocki	17:30 18:40		1	10	4
34	Oct 17	25203	Woodman	11:50 12:55		1	05	5
35	Oct 18	25203	Potocki	10:50 12:00	+1.0	1	10	6
36	Oct 19	25203	Woodman	15:55 17:10	.95	1	15	7
37	Oct 27	25204	Potocki	12:20 13:30		1	10	1
38	Oct 27	25202	Potocki	15:45 16:50	1.5	1	05	18
39	Oct 29	25202	Potocki	10:05 10:50	1.7	0	45	19
40	Oct 29	25202	Potocki	15:55 16:40	1.8	0	45	20
41	Oct 31	25203	Cope	12:10 13:10		1	00	8
42	Nov 7	25203	Cope	10:25 11:35		1	10	9
43	Nov 8	25202	Potocki	15:30 16:40		1	10	21
44[2]	Nov 11	25202	Potocki	9:45 11:00	1.98	1	15	22*

*Suffered landing accident

Flight Test No.	Date	Aircraft No.	Pilot	Time of Lift-off & Touchdown	Max. Speed Flown in Mach #	Flight Duration Hrs/Min		Aircraft Flight
45	Nov 22	25204	Potocki	15:05 16:10		1	05	2
46	Nov 30	25204	Potocki	12:25 13:35	1.2	1	10	3
47	Dec 11	25201	Potocki	10:00 11:10		1	10	13
48	Dec 15	25201	Potocki	14:40 16:05		1	25	14
49	Dec 20	25201	Potocki	10:45 12:10		1	25	15
50	Dec 21	25201	Potocki	12:35 13:20		0	45	16
	(1959)							
51	Jan 5	25201	Potocki	11:25 12:25		1	00	17
52	Jan 5	25201	Potocki	16:00 16:45		0	45	18
53	Jan 11	25205	Potocki	15:45 16:25		0	40	1
54	Jan 17	25201	Potocki	11:00 12:00		1	00	19
55	Jan 20	25203	Potocki	12:25 13:20	1.7	0	55	10
56	Jan 24	25201	Woodman	11:30 12:35		1	05	20
57	Jan 27	25201	Potocki	16:15 17:15		1	00	21
58	Jan 31	25201	Potocki	13:45 14:30		0	45	22
59	Jan 31	25201	Potocki	16:55 17:35		0	40	23
60	Feb 1	25203	Woodman	10:55 12:10		1	15	11
61	Feb 2	25204	Cope	12:00 13:10		1	10	4
62	Feb 3	25204	Potocki	11:50 13:05		1	15	5
63	Feb 7	25204	Potocki	11:05 12:15	1.5	1	10	6
64	Feb 7	25201	Potocki	15:55 16:55	1.3	1	00	24
65	Feb 19	25203	Potocki	10:15 11:25		1	10	12
66	Feb 19	25201	Potocki	13:35 14:25	1.75	0	50	25

[1]Highest speed flown by Jan Zurakowski   [2]Highest speed flown in program — Spud Potocki

INDIVIDUAL PILOT FLIGHT LOG FOR THE
AVRO CF-105 "ARROW"

JAN ZURAKOWSKI "ZURA"

Aircraft Flight No.	Date	Aircraft No.	Flying Time Hrs/Min		NOTES
1	25 Mar/58	25201	0	35	Initial flight. (Speeds up to 250 kt and altitude to 11,000 ft)
2	1 Apr/58	25201	0	50	(Nosewheel failed to retract. Flight restricted to handling below 250 kt.)
3	3 Apr/58	25201	1	05	M:1-1
4	15 Apr/58	25201	1	15	T.R.U. Unserviceable rendering telemetry inoperative. No high speed work
5	17 Apr/58	25201	1	10	Undercarriage snag after 'g' pull at 450 kt. Aborted high speed briefing
6	18 Apr/58	25201	0	55	M:1.25
7	18 Apr/58	25201	0	40	M:1.52 at 49,000 ft. Height of 50,000 ft reached
10	7 June/58	25201	1	45	Damper troubles at take off. Nose undercarriage door stuck down
11	11 June/58	25201	1	20	Aircraft damaged on landing. Port gear lengthening mechanism unserviceable
		(Sub Total	9	35)	
1	1 Aug/58	25202	1	35	Initial flight. 30,000 ft.
2	23 Aug/58	25202	1	00	M:1-5. Damper checks
3	26 Aug/58	25202	1	05	M:1-62
4	26 Aug/58	25202	1	00	M:1-7
5	27 Aug/58	25202	1	05	Ottawa telemetry check. M:1-5
7	28 Aug/58	25202	1	20	Ottawa telemetry check. M:1-72
8	14 Sept/58	25202	1	05	Damper handling. Telemetry unserviceable
9	14 Sept/58	25202	1	10	Damper checking. M:1-86 at 50,000 ft
10	16 Sept/58	25202	1	10	2-2 'g'. M:1-2 and damper check. Dutch roll investigation
11	26 Sept/58	25202	1	05	Pitch damper check. Subsonic
12	26 Sept/58	25202	1	00	M:1-55
		(Sub Total	12	35)	
1	22 Sept/58	25203	1	35	Initial flight. M:1-2
		(Sub Total	1	35)	**Grand total 23 hrs 45 mins**

PETER COPE

Aircraft Flight No.	Date	Aircraft No.	Flying Time Hrs/Min		NOTES
16	3 Oct/58	25202	1	05	Familiarization. M:1-5
		(Sub total	1	05)	
3	6 Oct/58	25203	1	00	Performance 1A tailcones up to M:1-7 at 50,000 ft
8	31 Oct/58	25203	1	00	Utility hydraulic failure. Gear down flight
9	7 Nov/58	25203	1	10	Fuel consumption at 35,000 ft and single engine checks.
		(Sub Total	3	10)	
4	2 Feb/59	25204	1	10	Check flight–directed to Trenton
		(Sub Total	1	10)	**Grand total 5 hrs 25 mins**

F/LT. JACK WOODMAN R.C.A.F.

Aircraft Flight No.	Date	Aircraft No.	Flying Time Hrs/Min		NOTES
8	22 Apr/58	25201	1	10	Familiarization. M:1-4
20	24 Jan/59	25201	1	05	RCAF damper system check. Low level only due to weather
		(Sub Total	2	15)	
13	28 Sept/58	25202	0	55	M:1-7 at 50,000 ft. RCAF handling
		(Sub Total	0	55)	
5	17 Oct/58	25203	1	05	Undercarriage door trouble starboard side. Low speed P.E.s with F-86
7	19 Oct/58	25203	1	15	Partial P.E.s, aborted high speed checks due to red light at M:0-95
11	1 Feb/59	25203	1	15	RCAF damper check
		(Sub Total	3	35)	**Grand total 6 hrs 45 mins**

		W. "SPUD" POTOCKI			
Aircraft Flight No.	Date	Aircraft No.	Flying Time Hrs/Min		NOTES
9	23 Apr/58	25201	0	45	Familiarization. M:1-2
12	5 Oct/58	25201	1	20	Acceptance (test) from production shop after repair. Subsonic
13	11 Dec/58	25201	1	10	Gear down–main door up check flight. Modified elevator controls
14	15 Dec/58	25201	1	25	Damper checks–restricted due to gear unsafe indication
15	20 Dec/58	25201	1	25	Continuation of damper checks.
16	21 Dec/58	25201	0	45	As flight No. 15
17	5 Jan/59	25201	1	00	Damper system check, 20,000 ft
18	5 Jan/59	25201	0	45	Extension ASI to 650 kt at 17,000 ft
19	17 Jan/59	25201	1	00	Damper system checks and elevator hinge moment
21	27 Jan/59	25201	1	00	General damper handling
22	31 Jan/59	25201	0	45	Extension of flight envelope
23	31 Jan/59	25201	0	40	Extension of flight envelope
24	7 Feb/59	25201	1	00	Climb stick tape. Roll and sideslip investigation up to M:1-3
25	19 Feb/59	25201	0	50	Last Arrow flight M 1.75 @ 35,000 ft.
		(Sub Total	13	50)	
6	25 Aug/58	25202	1	05	Damper handling. M:1-7
14	28 Sept/58	25202	0	45	M:1-55. 3 'g'. 1-3 at 36,000 ft. Pitch oscillation ± 3 'g'
15	3 Oct/58	25202	1	25	Pitch oscillation investigation
17	5 Oct/58	25202	0	50	All dampers up to M:1-45. 500 kt at 9,000 ft. Undercarriage doors open.
18	27 Oct/58	25202	1	05	Max speed 500 kt IAS at 7,500 ft on pivot door check.
19	29 Oct/58	25202	0	45	Flutter check. M:1-7
20	29 Oct/58	25202	0	45	Flutter check. M:1-8
21	8 Nov/58	25202	1	10	Assessment of modified elevator. Parallel servo and feel trim to rear not satisfactory
22	11 Nov/58	25202	1	15	Stbd U/C collapsed during the landing run.
		(Sub Total	9	05)	
2	1 Oct/58	25203	0	45	Snag clearance. M:1-7
4	16 Oct/58	25203	1	10	Fuel consumption and level speed checks at 35,000 ft. Subsonic
6	18 Oct/58	25203	1	10	Level speeds and fuel consumption. Supersonic on climb
10	20 Jan/59	25203	0	55	Check flight to M:1-7 with modified elevator system. Aircraft turbine seized
12	19 Feb/59	25203	1	10	Damper optimization. Observer D.E. Darrah carried.
		(Sub Total	5	10)	
1	27 Oct/58	25204	1	10	Initial flight–gear down 250 kt maximum
2	22 Nov/58	25204	1	05	Check flight
3	30 Nov/58	25204	1	10	Continuation of snag clearance to M:1-2
5	3 Feb/59	25204	1	15	Gear down ferry to base
6	7 Feb/59	25204	1	10	Clearance flight–limited to M:1-5 by pedal judder
		(Sub Total	5	50)	
1	11 Jan/59	25205	0	40	Initial flight gear down
		(Sub Total	0	40)	Grand total 34 hrs 35 mins

TOTAL FLIGHTS AND FLYING TIMES OF EACH AIRCRAFT

Aircraft No.	Flight	Total Time Hrs/Min	
25201	25	25	40
25202	22	23	40
25203	12	13	30
25204	6	7	00
25205	1	0	40
TOTAL	66	70	30

SUMMARY OF AVRO CF-105 "ARROW" FLIGHT PROGRAM

Aircraft No.	Number of Flights	Pilot	Total Time Airborne Hrs/Min
25201	9	J. Zurakowski	9 35
	14	W. Potocki	13 50
	2	F/Lt. J. Woodman	2 15
25202	11	J. Zurakowski	12 35
	9	W. Potocki	9 05
	1	P. Cope	1 05
	1	F/Lt. J. Woodman	0 55
25203	1	J. Zurakowski	1 35
	5	W. Potocki	5 10
	3	P. Cope	3 10
	3	F/Lt. J. Woodman	3 35
25204	5	W. Potocki	5 50
	1	P. Cope	1 10
25205	1	W. Potocki	0 40

AVRO CF-105 ARROW AIRCRAFT DATA

	Arrow 1	Arrow 2	Arrow 2A	Arrow 3
Length	80ft. 10in.	85ft. 6in.	85ft. 6in.	85ft. 6in.
Wing span	50ft.	50ft.	50ft.	50ft.
Empty Weight	49,040 lb.	45,000 lb.	45,000 lb.	45,000 lb
Normal Gross Weight	57,000 lb.	62,431 lb.	62,431 lb.	62,500 lb.
Max. Gross Weight	68,602 lb.	68,847 lb.	68,847 lb.	70,000 lb.
Fuel capacity	2,897 gal.	3,297 gal.	3,297 gal.	3,297 gal.
Engines-Type	Pratt-Whitney J-75 P-5	Orenda PS-13 Iroquois 2	Iroquois 2	Iroquois 3
Base thrust	12,500 lb.	19,250 lb.	19,250 lb.	21,000 lb.
Thrust with afterburner	18,500 lb.	26,000 lb.	26,000 lb.	30,000 lb.
Max. Speed (40,000 ft.)	1,325mph (M2.0)	1,325mph	1,325mph	2,000mph
Combat Speed	Mach 1.5	Mach 1.5	Mach 1.5	Mach 2.5
Cruise Speed	Mach 0.92	Mach 0.92	Mach 0.92	Mach 1.0
Combat ceiling	53,000ft.	58,500ft.	58,600ft.	68,600ft.
Climb rate — from S.L.	38,450ft/min.	44,500ft./min.	44,500ft./min.	classified
—from 40,000ft.	16,500ft/min.	20,300ft/min.	20,300ft/min.	classified
Combat Radius—high speed	----	264 mi.	575 mi.	487 mi.
—max. range	----	408 mi.	787 mi.	593 mi.

Many of these figures are estimated

First officially released photo of the Iroquois engine — the planned powerplant for Arrow 2 aircraft.

6

Iroquois Engine and Flight Testing on B-47

To attempt to describe the complexity and technical achievement of the Iroquois jet engine, in one short chapter, is impossible! It would require a great amount of space to merely inform the reader adequately of the components within the engine itself. We will simply attempt to give an idea in reasonably simple terms, of what was achieved in design and test operations during the short life of the Iroquois program.

Iroquois Design and Development

A decision was made in 1953, by Avro Gas Turbine Division (later Orenda Engines), to design an engine to power the successor of the CF-100 and to bypass the next generation in the normal development of jet engines; this would make a very significant leap forward in the 'state of the art'. Starting in the Spring of 1953, a series of aerodynamic and performance studies, and mechanical design layouts culminated in a design proposal being approved by the Hawker Siddley Group Design Council, which visited Malton in September 1953. Originally the project was known as PS13 (project study), and was without military sponsorship.

This was undertaken as a private venture by Avro, Canada. The resulting PS13, (later called the Iroquois) was to power the (yet unnamed) Avro Canada CF-105 'Arrow'.

The Iroquois concept was based on the RCAF requirement for an interceptor which called for a maximum performance of Mach 1.5 at 50,000 feet.

The specification also called for a rather stringent condition for standby operation of the aircraft. It was specified that with the aircraft standing at "readiness" (pilot in the cockpit but engines not running) it could be airborne in 60 seconds maximum.

This posed a considerable challenge in aerodynamic, thermo-dynamic and mechanical design as well as manufacturing technology.

In just 20 days the engine design team produced the basic layout; an engine with two compressors, twin-spool with an integral afterburner with modulated nozzle, designed to have a thrust-to-weight ratio of better than 5:1 and to produce a sea-level* dry thrust of 19,250 lb. (26,000 lb. with afterburner).

*The term "dry thrust" is used by aeronautical engineers to state performance of a jet engine that has an afterburner installed, but not lit during the testing.

The engine had a 3-stage axial, low pressure (L.P.) compressor, driven by a single-stage turbine; and a seven-stage, high-pressure (H.P.) compressor driven by a two-stage turbine. An annular vaporizing type combustion chamber was incorporated. The engine was the first to use a transonic first stage in the L.P. compressor, and to dispense with inlet guide vanes. It was probably the first jet engine to utilize an overhung, low-pressure compressor supported by the low-pressure rotor through an inter-rotor bearing. This allowed the two rotors to be supported by only two bearing support structures, a design which had never been tried before!

The Orenda design team realized at the outset that the utmost enterprise would be demanded to stay within the weight limit imposed, if they were to achieve the 5 to 1 power weight ratio.

Initially, 'titanium' offered the greatest single

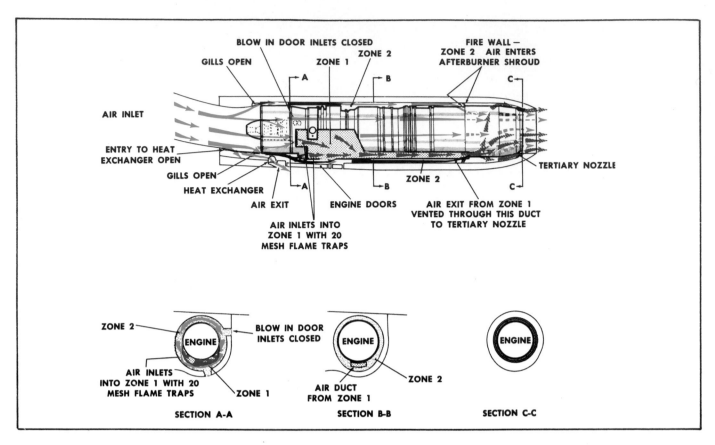

Engine cooling — flight case Mach 0.5 and upwards.

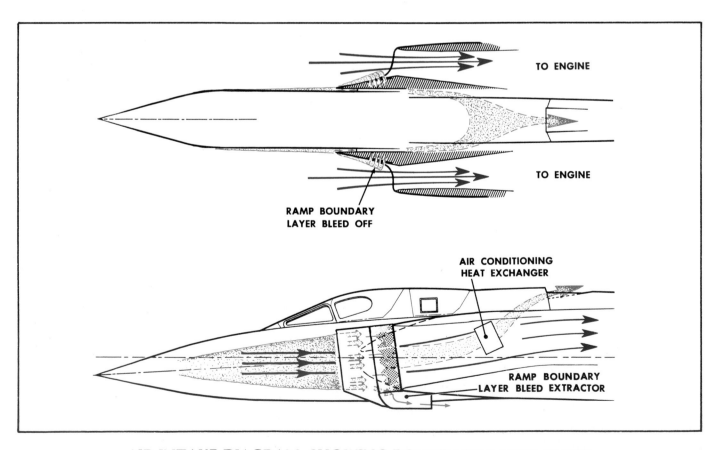

AIR INTAKE DIAGRAM, SHOWING BOUNDARY LAYER BLEED.

opportunity for keeping the weight down. Using it to replace aluminum in the front end of the engine, it was estimated that the engine would be 850 pounds lighter than if steel was used. The other weight saving design solution was the two-spool compressor arrangement which was lighter than a single unit designed for the same duty, with the added advantage that the two-spool design was more flexible in engine performance and handling characteristics. The combustion chamber was made smaller, and consequently lighter, as a result the airflow velocities were increased considerably over normal practice without penalizing the combustion performance.

While the metal 'titanium' appeared to be attractive material as a weight saver, there were many challenges to be overcome, before it could be used in production. The material was in short supply, and the lack of knowledge of it's physical properties and fabrication techniques had to be overcome. It was also very expensive, relative to the more common materials such as steel and aluminum. In 1951, there was only 150 lbs. produced, which grew to 2,000 lbs. in 1953. Though the output in future years grew dramatically, there was not enough to satisfy demand. However, Orenda was able to obtain sufficient material for 12 engine sets.

On the design side, the picture was bright, while some weight saving could be obtained by exchanging a steel part for a titanium part it was recognized that if the engine part was designed in titanium at the outset then the supporting structure could also be lightened with a greater total weight saving overall. This also eased the design problems associated with the rotor bearing.

The stator rings, i.e. those carrying the stationary compressor blades constituted a potential rubbing area for the compressor blade tips. These rings were converted to steel to eliminate a fire hazard. Titanium is a poor heat conductor and experience showed that where a local hot spot developed, it could result in a hole burning through the material. With the air from the compressor bleeding through the hole, there might be a blowtorch effect created which could endanger the entire aircraft structure.

When installed in the Arrow, the Iroquois engine had its own cooling system; the automatic intake gills immediately adjacent to the compressor inlet opened up when a speed greater than Mach 0.5 was attained. This allowed air to by-pass around the engine for cooling purposes and to minimize spillage at the intakes at supersonic speeds, and still produced good performance with fixed geometry intakes in the subsonic, transonic and supersonic ranges.

This by-pass air, cooled the compartment walls and the afterburner duct and gave additional thrust by the use of ejectors on the exit nozzle.

In early 1955 there came a reminder of the high stakes being played for by the developing of titanium blades. Checks were made after each engine run had been carried out and, it was found that small cracks were developing in many of the blades!

This problem was traced to excess hydrogen in the raw material which weakened the titanium. This was an impurity of 140 parts per million, rather than 25 parts per million. To salvage the material and blades, it was found that the hydrogen could be successfully bubbled out of the metal by being degassed at a high temperature in a vacuum.

Another major breakthrough was achieved by the International Nickel Company which developed a high temperature alloy that could be cast rather than forged into turbine blade shapes. This new alloy could operate 25°F higher in metal temperature compared to the air-cooled blade temperature which was being developed. Thus the air-cooled turbine blade program was cancelled and the new alloy adopted with the resultant simpler design.

The final detailed design was completed on May 1, 1954 and the first light-up of the Iroquois was achieved on December 15, 1954. This was an incredible performance in the role of design, development and manufacture of such a complex and advance jet engine. Full credit must go to the outstanding Orenda Iroquois engine team, led by Charles A. Grinyer, Vice President and Chief Engineer; consisting of: F.H. (Harry) Keast, Assistant Chief Engineer (technical), Dr. A. Muraszew, Chief Experimental Engineer, and B.A. (Burt) Avery, Chief Design Engineer.

Significant performance achievements were recorded in Dec. 1955, just one year after the first running. A maximum thrust in excess of 19,000 lbs. was recorded during a sustained run at maximum speed. Indications were that high speed operation was satisfactory both aerodynamically and mechanically.

On June 24, 1956, the first official 50 hour Pre-Flight Rating Test (P.F.R.T.) was successfully carried out. The afterburner operated for the first time July 3. By September 19, engine development

IROQUOIS DEVELOPMENT PROGRAM.

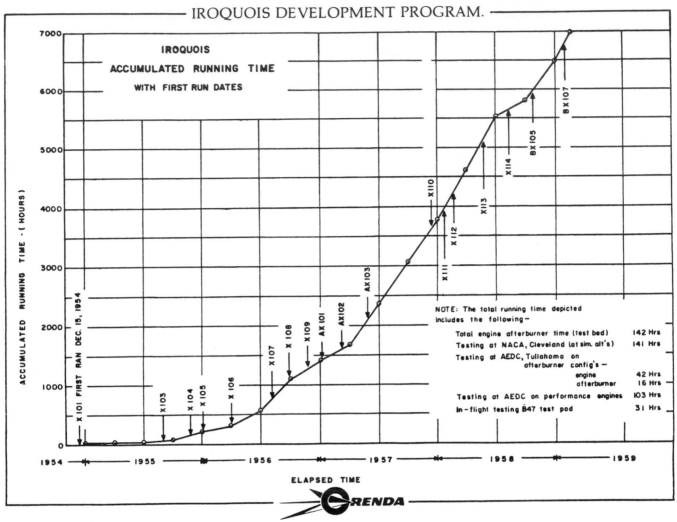

IROQUOIS
ACCUMULATED RUNNING TIME
WITH FIRST RUN DATES

NOTE: The total running time depicted includes the following—

Total engine afterburner time (test bed)	142 Hrs
Testing at NACA, Cleveland (at sim. alt's)	141 Hrs
Testing at AEDC, Tullahoma on afterburner config's —	
engine	42 Hrs
afterburner	16 Hrs
Testing at AEDC on performance engines	103 Hrs
In-flight testing B47 test pod	31 Hrs

ACCUMULATED RUNNING TIME - (HOURS)

ELAPSED TIME

ORENDA

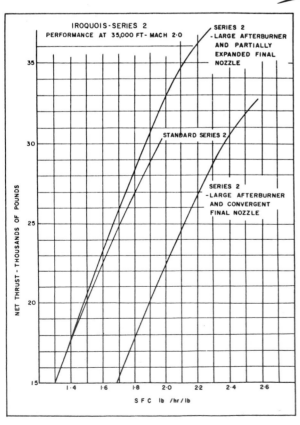

IROQUOIS-SERIES 2
PERFORMANCE AT 35,000 FT - MACH 2·0

SERIES 2
- LARGE AFTERBURNER AND PARTIALLY EXPANDED FINAL NOZZLE

STANDARD SERIES 2

SERIES 2
- LARGE AFTERBURNER AND CONVERGENT FINAL NOZZLE

NET THRUST - THOUSANDS OF POUNDS

S F C lb /hr/lb

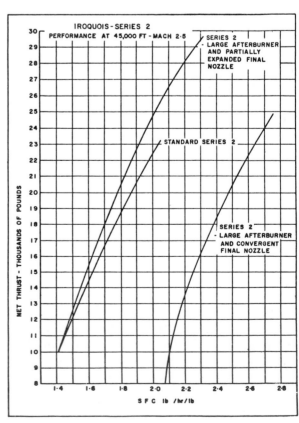

IROQUOIS-SERIES 2
PERFORMANCE AT 45,000 FT - MACH 2·5

SERIES 2
- LARGE AFTERBURNER AND PARTIALLY EXPANDED FINAL NOZZLE

STANDARD SERIES 2

SERIES 2
- LARGE AFTERBURNER AND CONVERGENT FINAL NOZZLE

NET THRUST - THOUSANDS OF POUNDS

S F C lb /hr/lb

running time had reached 1000 hours.

By early 1957, the many aerodynamic and mechanical "unknowns" of the original design had been virtually eliminated and modification of a B-47 bomber, which had been allocated by the United States Air Force to the RCAF for Orenda's use, was going ahead. The plan was to have a seventh engine pod installed on the right rear side of the fuselage below the tailplane.

During this period, further test facilities required for the program were being constructed. These facilities consisted mainly of new development test cells, a high altitude engine test facility, and full scale afterburner and rotating blade cooling test rigs.

Meantime, arrangements were being made for simulated high altitude running tests at the National Advisory Committee for Aeronautical laboratories in the United States, and for cold weather testing at the National Research Council laboratories in Ottawa.

As general mechanical reliability continued to improve at the expected rate, so further milestones were passed. On July 27, 1957, the first official 100 hour endurance test was successfully carried out at a reduced thrust rating of 18,750 lbs.

A demonstration run at over 19,000 lbs. dry thrust was carried out for Canadian Government representatives on November 1st, 1957 and 12 days later, the Iroquois was run, at altitude in the B-47 for the first time.

A high point was reached in January 1958, when the first phase of testing at simulated altitude and forward speed conditions was completed at the NACA laboratories in Cleveland, Ohio. The engine was run successfully for two hours in an atmosphere heated to over 240° F. with a peak of five minutes at 349°F (equivalent to Mach. 2.3).

Over 100 hours running was achieved during this test phase during which time the Iroquois recorded what was probably the highest dry thrust ever achieved by a turbojet on the North American continent. An Orenda-patented relight method proved entirely successful, giving normal relights at designed Mach numbers up to 60,000 feet, the altitude capability of the tunnel.

At this point the Iroquois had completed more than 5,000 hours of bench running. In addition, many thousands of hours more had been accumulated in rig-testing such principal components as the main bearings, compressors, combustion and after-burner systems, at the Orenda test establishment at Nobel (Ontario) near Parry Sound.

Iroquois Flight Testing on B-47

Phase one of the Arrow program consisted of five Arrows equipped with off the shelf J-75 engines. In phase two, the Iroquois would replace the J-75 and become the Arrow's standard powerplant. During the development of the Iroquois engine, the Company started looking around for a suitable aircraft to use as a flying test bed. There were not many aircraft around that could handle an extra engine of the Iroquois size and with the power that the engine produced.

The thrust was enormous for an engine of that time, (1958), 19,350 lbs. dry on the test bed, and over 25,600 lbs. with afterburner. These are actual figures recorded on the engine during its 50 hour test. The specifications called for 19,250 lbs. dry and 26,000 lbs. with afterburner.

The acceleration was nothing short of fantastic. It could go from idle to full thrust in 2.8 seconds and if you selected idle to afterburner, then it would go up to full thrust; the afterburner would light; the final nozzle would arrange itself and stabilize 4.5 seconds from initial throttle opening. Remember! the engine was still being developed!

It was decided that the B-47 would be the best airplane to use to flight test the Iroquois. Some mention should be made here of the willing and generous co-operation of United States authorities in connection with the Iroquois program. This consisted of provision of time in U.S. engine test facilities until Orenda's own facilities came into operation; and the loan of a United States Air Force six engine B-47 jet bomber, complete with related servicing equipment and the training of Orenda personal to service and fly the U.S. aircraft.

This showed not only a good co-operation between the two countries, but a keen interest in the Arrow Project in the U.S. at that time. The aircraft was duly delivered to Canadair at Montreal, by a crew from the Strategic Air Force training base in Wichita, for installation of the Iroquois pod on the right side just under the tailplane. It was quite a large nacelle being some 30 feet long and about 6 feet in diameter. It was located quite a bit off the centre line of the aircraft and therefore the engine thrust line was not in line with that of the aircraft.Ideally it would have been best toed in slightly but instead of this, it was

B-47 crew consisting of Len Hobbs, pilot; Johnny McLaughlin, flight engineer; with Chief Test Pilot Mike Cooper—Slipper, on ladder.

toed outward which gave asymetric problems of control with the aircraft during Iroquois flight testing.

Canadair Montreal did the job of modification with a dummy engine and put in the necessary systems and controls for the engine, with racks, etc. in the bomb bay for the sophisticated instrumentation equipment. During this time Mike Cooper-Slipper, an Avro test pilot had been joined with another pilot, Len Hobbs, who came over from the U.K. and Johnny McLaughlin a flight engineer who had worked on the Orenda program. This 3 man flight crew went to the U.S. Air Force Strategic Air Command (SAC) Training Base in Wichita. This was quite a concession for the U.S. Military; to let 3 Canadians, especially civilians, join U.S. Air Force personnel as a regular B-47 crew on a highly classified aircraft. It was also the time of the Suez Crisis. Mike Cooper-Slipper was trained as a regular SAC Commander ready to go into a squadron. The Canadian crew had nothing but praise and admiration for the way the training was carried out and after 10 weeks emerged as a fully qualified B-47 crew. The crew consisted of the flight engineer, located in the nose of the aircraft and the two pilots who were situated in tandem with dual controls. They could now fly in all weather and with ground control approach landing down to zero-zero visibility. The airplane itself was something quite different to what they were used to flying. It had six jet engines with a highly swept wing, that was very flexible; it had a bicycle undercarriage—two main gear — one forward and one aft with one outrigger on each wing. This brought in a completely new set of problems and a new way of flying. Canadair got the job finished and put ballast in to compensate for the tail engine. They had to get the centre of gravity correct as the B-47 was very sensitive to this.

The modified aircraft then departed for Malton, which in itself was a major triumph as the take off was a one shot deal; because the short runways at Canadair (Cartierville) left no room to abort the take-off. Liftoff was uneventful, although filled with anticipation. The landing at Malton was very rough, according to Mike. The pod on the rear end, had changed the aircraft characteristics quite a bit. On getting closer to the ground, the ground effect of the rear pod became very apparent and caused a lifting action.

The initial design of the Iroquois had commenced on September 14, 1953 and was completed May 1, 1954 and first light-up achieved on December 15, 1954. Whenever the Arrow is discussed the enormous costs involved are never far behind. It is interesting to note that although the costs of developing any new engine are high, the Iroquois costs were not unreasonable. The Iroquois had passed its 50 hour flight rating test, which of course permitted Orenda to test fly the engine in the B-47, at a cost of somewhere around 90 million dollars. It was heading towards the 150 hour final qualification test at an estimated additional cost of another 9 to 10 million dollars. By comparison, figures of the J-75 development showed that at its 50 hour test point, it had cost approximately 278 million dollars. It can be seen from this, that Orenda had reached the same point for about a third of the cost.

The Iroquois weighed about 4,500 lbs. including about 1,400 lbs. of titanium, a saving of about 700 lbs. and thereby justified the use of it in the engine. Orenda was pretty well pioneering in the field of titanium, but gambled, that they could make it work. Unfortunately, the high altitude ground test facilities in which the engine could be run at simulated high altitude and pressures experienced at 50,000 feet to 60,000 feet, was not available. It had been planned to be used in conjunction with the flight test program. As a result all altitude testing had to be done on the B-47. There were a few minor problems with the Iroquois and the B-47. On one occasion, there was an explosion in flight with the engine. The trouble occurred about 50 miles north of Malton, near Barrie, Ontario. the B-47 was starting to climb with full Iroquois power on (this was the only recorded occasion that the Iroquois was put to full throttle while in flight test). Suddenly there was an enormous bang and the whole aircraft shook, followed by a deadly silence. The pilot's position was a long way from the Iroquois but dust flew up into the cockpit. The Iroquois was immediately shut down and its fire extinguishers pulled. The vibration diminished as the engine came to a stop.

The CF-100 chase pilot came close by to look at the pod and reported lots of smoke but no fire. It goes without saying that the B-47 returned to base rather quickly with a few anxious moments thrown in. What had happened upon inspection was that a blade had failed and pieces had penetrated the nacelle of the Iroquois and entered the rear fuselage of the B-47. Fortunately there was no major damage to the aircraft. The problem was later rectified by a change in blade design and manufacture.

The Iroquois obtained a total (in flight)

B-47's first arrival at Malton from Cartierville, Que.

Aircraft being serviced.

View of engine pod on rear fuselage of B-47.

Iroquois engine, installed in B-47, undergoing engine runs at Avro test cells.

Rear cockpit of B-47 showing additional throttle for Iroquois engine.

B-47 over Malton, Iroquois engine mounting clearly discernible.

B-47 with day-glow paint and Canadian Airforce marking
(the B-47 was designated a CL-52 during its stay in Canada).

Rear view of test bed for Iroquois engine showing large nacelle.

running time on the B-47 of 31 hours before cancellation.

Considerable knowledge was gained regarding reliability through the flight test program. Confirmation of turbine tip clearance requirements was obtained through altitude relight investigation. Altitude testing had shown that for supersonic regions where intake buzz could be a problem, the Iroquois had plenty of surge margin both in the LP and HP compressors. Inlet flow distortions at the LP compressor up to 14% were acceptable. Light-up at altitude was excellent. This was accomplished by an oxygen assisted system, which was unique in the industry.

In January 1959 engine X113 completed a 50 hour Pre-Flight Training Test. Operation and handling during the test was very good. There was only negligible deterioration in performance between the initial and final rating curve. The test was completed in 88 hours, 43 minutes running time. It included 90 starts and many slam accelerations. The mechanical condition of the engine after test was good. It is interesting to note that when the B-47 was in flight, one of the B-47's engines had to be kept running at full power to offset the asymetric thrust of the Iroquois and another to keep the hydraulic electric services etc, running, but progressively the balance of the engines could be closed down. It was not possible to open up all seven engines to full power.

The existing Series 2 Iroquois was designed for Mach 2.0 capabilities but could have been raised to Mach 2.5 very easily as the only limiting items were the last three stages of the compressor. Here, the material properties of the titanium used were not adequate for the H.P. compressor's outlet temperature. The material would need to be changed to an advanced titanium having better high temperature properties or as an alternative, steel. A Mach 2.5 version with a high rated afterburner could have been provided as the aircraft fuselage would have permitted an increase in diameter or lengthening of the afterburner, or both, to allow an increase in the afterburner thrust.

Initial flight testing had been carried out in the modified B-47 bomber simultaneously with extensive running under conditions of simulated altitude environments in high altitude engine test cells. Final proving of the engine would have been done in an Avro CF-105 Arrow, where the full potential of the engine could be exploited.

On December 17, 1958 the first preproduction engine was delivered to Avro, the second following on December 21st. In mid-February 1959 Iroquois engine #115 (L.H.) and engine #116 (R.H.) were being readied for Arrow 206. On February 20, 1959, Black Friday, the contract was cancelled!

The performance of the engine at that time (1959) over 31 years ago, completely justified the faith of those who put the project in motion and proved the theory of the original concept. It should be realized that only today are engines routinely achieving the same thrust and performance as the Iroquois did those many years ago. There were also developments planned which would have increased its rated thrust by at least 33 1/3%, therefore, the Iroquois was ideally suited for any mission which called for supersonic speeds in a fighter, bomber, interceptor, or possibly a missile. By dropping the afterburner and derating the engine for increased reliability, engine life and lower fuel consumption, a first-class powerplant would have been available for civilian jet liner application.

Future tests were being planned for the Iroquois engine in the high altitude facilities to investigate its performance over a wide spectrum of speed and altitude. These planned tests could well have been a rehearsal for Mach 3 at 100,000 feet.

Shortly after cancellation, technicians from the Boeing factory arrived at Malton to help with the removal of the test Iroquois from the rear of the B-47 and return the B-47 to its normal condition so that the aircraft could be returned to the United States. Not generally known is that when Mike Cooper-Slipper and his crew returned the B-47 to Davis Monthan Air Force Base near Tuscon, Arizona, and during their short stay, a few important parts were removed from the aircraft. Then both wings were cut off and the fuselage cut in half, the pieces fed into a large smelter.

Two Iroquois engines still survive — one may be viewed at the National Aviation Museum, Ottawa and the other, complete with afterburner, at Canadian Warplane Heritage Museum (CWHM), Hamilton. It may be the engine out of the B-47, as it has all the flight instrumentation still intact. Unfortunately, the compressor and turbine casing have been torched in two areas. Two of J-75s engines that were in the Arrows are also at CWHM. These engines were found stored in cans at Moncton, New Brunswick airport by an airline pilot.

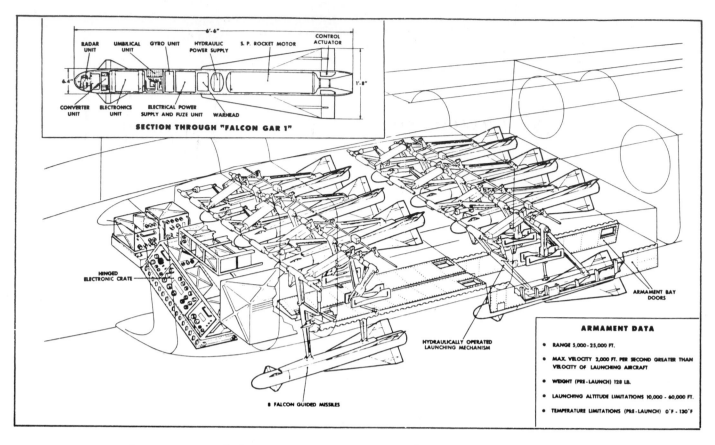

Armament and electronic equipment installations — Falcon Missiles.

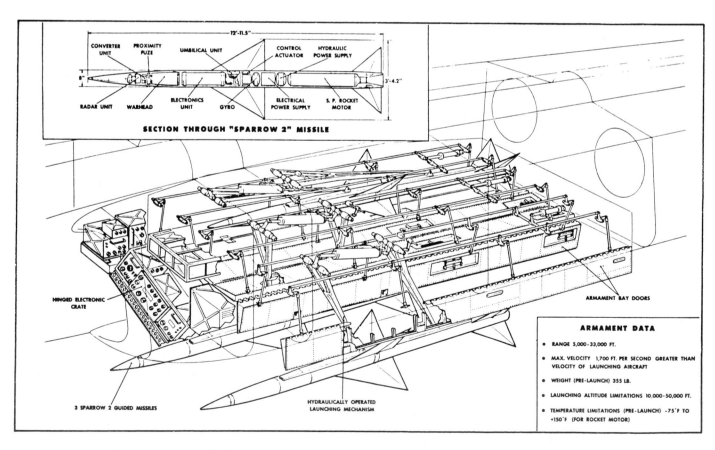

Armament and electronic equipment installations — Sparrow 2 Missiles.

Weapon System and Defense Strategy

Weapon System

The whole objective of the Arrow's development was a flying weapons system capable of intercepting and destroying a high speed bomber invading the northern part of the North American Continent, "CANADA".

The aircraft was the delivery system, and the electronic system and weapons were the search and destroy arms. This total weapons system that was to be developed for the Arrow, turned into the "Achilles Heel" of the whole program. The 'reason why' was the high demands of the Canadian Air Staff who wanted the moon! The system and missile that they insisted be developed, were far in advance of anything contemplated at that time and therefore, the projected price tag was enormous. The magnitude of these costs, when projected into production, and squadron service, exceeded the total cost of the aircraft development and procurement program. Thus the combined programs of the aircraft and its weapons quickly became too rich for the Canadian Government to fund.

To illustrate the snowball effect of the costs and complexities of the weapons system, it is worthwhile to briefly summarize some of its history and escalation. As Avro had previous experience with the Hughes Aircraft Company in the design and production of the weapons control system for their CF-100 Fighter, it was natural for AVRO to choose this company to build a readily available weapons control system and missiles. However in 1953, the Air Staff insisted that the production version of the Arrow must be able to accommodate the advanced Hughes MX-1179 system that was not yet developed. They also wanted bigger and better missiles than the proposed Falcons. The Air Staff in their wisdom decided that it would be nice if Canada could develop and build a marvellous new weapons system, custom built for the Arrow and much better than anything else contemplated. They also requested a new missile be developed called Sparrow 2.

To illustrate the disaster that was starting to emerge, a quote from Bill Gunston's book "Early Supersonic Fighters of the West", is worthwhile to show how the program went out of control:

"The new optimized fire control was called Astra 1. Major contractors were R.C.A. Victor, the Montreal associate of the giant R.C.A. Corporation, which unfortunately had little experience with avionics for fighters, and Honeywell Controls and Computing Devices of Canada. Astra 1 was planned as an all-can-do system of extreme sophistication. One could even agree that it ought to be better than anything else, if it ever came to fruition, but from the very beginning AVRO Aircraft was cast under a cloud of gloom. It was obvious that it could no longer control the program costs, and the potential costs of Astra 1 were enormous (before long the CF-105 team wryly suggested that the systems name was short for 'Astronomically Expensive'). In 1956 AVRO formally recommended the use of an improved Hughes system, but again found it difficult to marshall convincing arguments because the Astra 1 system was highly classified and had yet to overrun its budget or timing in a serious way...so AVRO continued to shrink from having a major

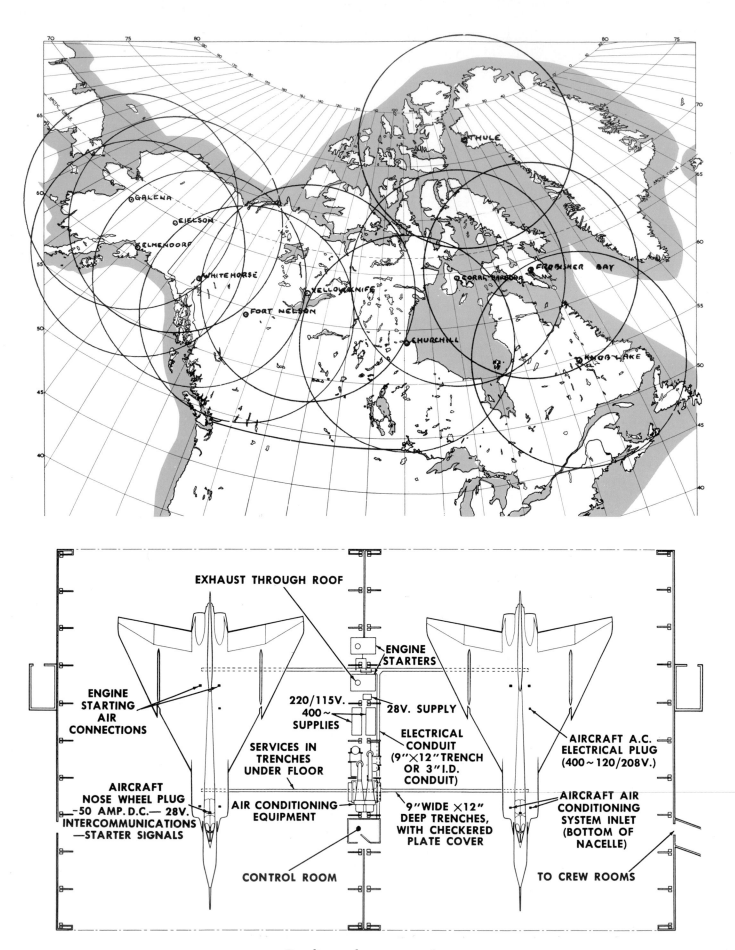

Readiness hangar study.

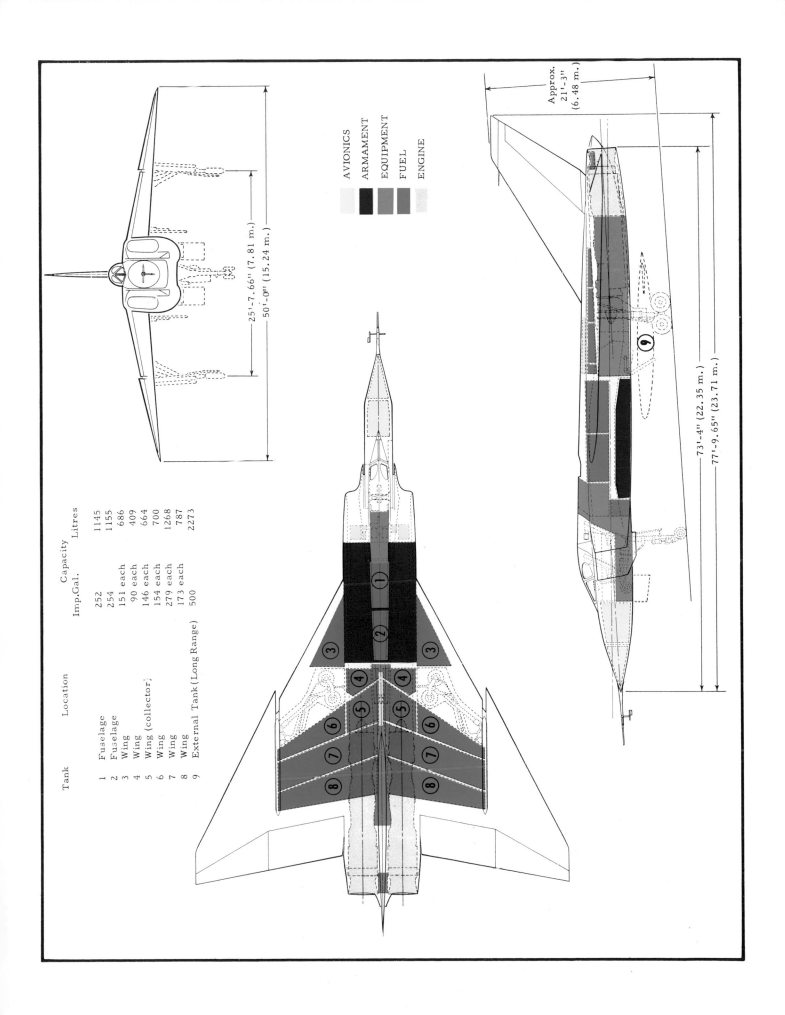

Tank	Location	Capacity	
		Imp.Gal.	Litres
1	Fuselage	252	1145
2	Fuselage	254	1155
3	Wing	151 each	686
4	Wing	90 each	409
5	Wing (collector)	146 each	664
6	Wing	154 each	700
7	Wing	279 each	1268
8	Wing	173 each	787
9	External Tank (Long Range)	500	2273

AVIONICS
ARMAMENT
EQUIPMENT
FUEL
ENGINE

25'-7.66" (7.81 m.)

50'-0" (15.24 m.)

Approx. 21'-3" (6.48 m.)

73'-4" (22.35 m.)

77'-9.65" (23.71 m.)

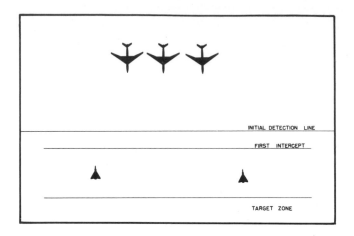

A narrow defence zone is capable of only limited defence and is easily saturated.

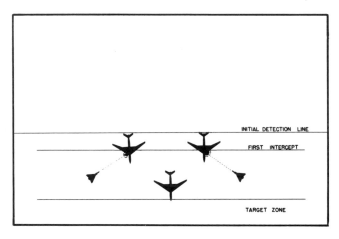

With a narrow defence zone some of the enemy may be destroyed but the inevitable saturation of the defences and the difficulty of bringing a large defensive effort to bear in a restricted range, would result in bombers getting through to the targets in effective numbers.

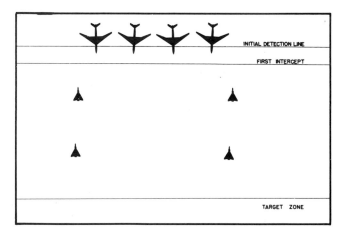

The defence zone with overlapping defensive areas would prove very costly to penetrate, and if of sufficient depth, could prove to be virtually incapable of saturation without the enemy risking a disproportionate number of bombers on a single raid.

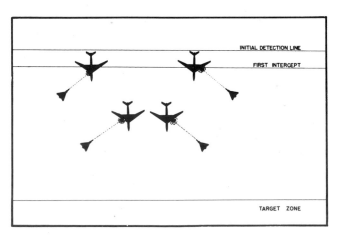

A deep defensive zone is difficult to saturate and is more adaptable to the support of effective waves of defensive aircraft.

For an effective defence, the defence system should have as great a depth as possible. Best results are obtained if the enemy is forced to attack through a long defence corridor and to fight every mile of the way to his target.

dispute with the customer on whom they depended for their entire income".

The story of the confusion and escalation of cost was further compounded by the Air Staff deciding to put the whole program and its cost control under the project management of the R.C.A.F.; Assistant for Arrow Weapons Systems (A/AWS). Therefore AVRO was now only a normal contractor for part of the program and had no way to control the overall cost.

These changes in requirements and complexities of the weapons system discussed above, had a major impact on the Arrow program, requiring major design and manufacturing changes, which increased the aircraft's total cost. One of the biggest, was the increase in diameter of the radar scanner dish, in the nose of the aircraft. It went from 23.5 to a final diameter of 38 inches. This increase in size in the nose to accommodate this large dish, in turn affected the directional stability of the aircraft; which in turn demanded a high degree of reliability out of the damping system, which was part of the Automatic Flight Control System. This has been discussed in a previous section called 'Fly-by-Wire'. It was integrated with the interceptor's fire control system making it completely automatic and controlled from the ground without the pilot having to do anything.

That was the Dream! But it was too much, too soon, causing the demise of a great program.

Defence Strategy
(Defence of North America)

The projected Air Defence of the North American Continent in the late 1950's and through the early 1960's presented some very difficult problems to Canadian Defence Staff.

Attacks to this region could be expected to be launched by two methods. The first method would be from naval vessels situated off both the eastern and western coastal areas. It was considered unlikely that surface craft would operate close to our shores because of the ease with which they could be detected and destroyed. Attacks from these areas would therefore most likely be by submarine launching of missiles of the type such as the Polaris missile. An airborne attack of any strength, by ship-based aircraft, was not considered likely because of the vulnerability of the large surface vessels required. The second method of attack to be expected would be an aerial attack from the North, most probably from a polar direction. Any attack from the South would be

extremely unlikely, owing to the lack of bases in this direction available to any major power.

It appears then that with the exception of submarine launched missiles requiring their own special mode of defence, the main attack to be expected would be an aerial attack across Alaska and northern Canada, aimed at the main industrial areas of the U.S.A. and southern areas of Ontario and Quebec.

For a defence area to be operationally useful, detection and surveillance of the enemy threat is a requirement. With the existing radar networks in operation in North America in 1958/59, an effective system of detection and surveillance was already in existence. The most Northerly of the radar chains — Distant Early Warning (D.E.W.) Line system, gave both an early warning of attack and a reasonable surveillance area.

The Avro Arrow being capable of either subsonic or supersonic defensive roles would require hard surface runways to operate from. In this northerly area, a number of Air Bases with suitable runways were already existing in a chain from coast to coast. When the operational range (620 n.m. radius subsonic operation) of the Arrow was centered on these existing bases one can see that considerable overlapping of defence areas was possible. These overlapping defence areas provided a defence zone over 1,000 miles in depth and ending well within the present Pine Tree defence area. Thus it would be possible to attack an enemy force over such a long line, as to make it extremely costly if not impractical, for this mode of attack to be used.

An Attack

Assuming an attack by 600 mph long range bombers and allowing five minutes from detection to scramble, the bomber force would be some fifty miles inside the D.E.W. Line at scramble. Intercept with the enemy threat would be made some 260 to 270 nautical miles south of the initial detection point. If the Arrow was restricted to a speed of Mach 0.9 this intercept was still well within the D.E.W. Line surveillance area. Second and third waves of Arrows could also be scrambled if there was an enemy threat remaining. The intercept distance would of course be reduced if a supersonic Arrow was available.

From the Iroquois test bed figures it was expected that the Arrow 2 at 'readiness' could start and be at full thrust in less than 20 seconds.

Black Friday,
February 20th, 1959

On Friday, February 20th, at about 11:00 a.m., the Prime Minister announced in the House of Commons termination of the Arrow and Iroquois Programs. At Avro, Toronto, at 11:20 a.m. approximately, the following announcement was made to all employees over the P/A system:

"The radio has recently announced that the Prime Minister stated in the House of Commons this morning that the Avro Arrow and Iroquois programs have been terminated. We, the Management of the Company, had no official information prior to this announcement being made. The Cancellation of the Arrow and the Iroquois has, however, been confirmed as a fact by Mr. Hore, the representative here of the Department of Defence Production. It is impossible at this stage to give you any further details until such time as I receive the official announcement from Ottawa. In the meantime, I would ask that you continue with your work. Later on in the day you will be informed as to our future."

At 12:22 p.m. the following termination instructions were received from the Department of Defence Production:

"Take notice that your contracts bearing reference numbers set out below including all amendments thereto are hereby termi-

nated as regards all supplies and services which have not been completed and shipped or performed thereunder prior to the receipt by you of this notice Stop You shall cease all work immediately, terminate subcontracts and orders, place no further subcontracts or orders and instruct all your subcontractors and suppliers to take similar action Stop You are requested to submit to the Department of Defence Production, Ottawa, Ontario, for consideration any claim which you may have as a result of this termination Stop Such claim and those of your subcontractors and suppliers, if any, are to be submitted on the prescribed departmental termination claim forms Stop On receipt of this notice, you should make application in writing to the Chief Settlement Officer, Department of Defence Production, Ottawa, for the requisite set of forms Stop Your claim and all correspondence conerning it should be addressed to..................Stop Ends

D.L. Thompson,
Dept. of Defence Production"

Sundry meetings of the management committee ensued and the following notice of termination was issued to all employees (excepting members of the senior management group):

"To All Employees:

#206 under final construction.

Arrow 206 alongside metal mockup moving down the final assembly line. Arrow's 207 and 208 are clearly visible flowing right behind Arrow 206.

The following statement was issued by Crawford Gordon, President and General Manager of A.V. Roe Canada Limited:

'Following the Prime Minister's statement we have received wires from the Government, instructing us to immediately cease all work on the Arrow and Iroquois programs at Malton and by all suppliers and subcontractors.

As a result, notice of termination of employment is being given to all employees of Avro Aircraft and Orenda Engines, pending a full assessment of the impact of the Prime Minister's statement on our aeronautical operations.

We profoundly regret this action but we have no alternative since the company received no prior notice of the decision and therefore we were unable to plan any orderly adjustment. The whole situation is and will be under constant review and when the full impact is determined a formal statement will be made by myself as soon as possible.'

All monthly, weekly, and hourly-paid employees are hereby given notice of lay-off as of this date and under the terms of the applicable collective agreements.

Tools must be returned to the Tool Cribs for clearance before final separation pay is made up. As all work on these projects is terminated, there will be no work for you to perform after this date. You may remove your tool boxes and your personal belongings on Monday, Tuesday and Wednesday, February 23, 24 and 25, during the regular day-shift working hours. Your separation pay, separation notice, vacation pay books etc., will be mailed as soon as possible.

Some employees will be required to perform termination functions and to maintain essential services. These employees will be notified by their supervisors and will report to work accordingly.

In the meantime, the company will assess the work available and the employees required. Those employees will be recalled or retained under the seniority provisions of the collective agreements.

(signed) J.L. Plant for
President and General Manager

When the termination notice was issued by Crawford Gordon, employees walked around in a state of disbelief. Many had expected that a scaling down of the Arrow program might occur, but an entire cancellation of the program left both the employees and management in a state of shock; it was totally unexpected.

The Company had no option; they were under contract and committed to various subcontractors to the tune of several millions of dollars of their own money, awaiting the Government's next fiscal year's appropriation. This was done with full knowledge and consent of the Government. The Company informed the Government of its decision to let an estimated 13-14,000 employees go, giving the Government an opportunity to come up with some kind of alternative, but no answer was forthcoming. There were five aircraft completed that had already flown and others virtually ready to roll off the assembly line, including the parts and components for virtually all 37 aircraft awaiting final assembly.

Shortly thereafter the Government ordered the Company to destroy or scrap anything and everything which related to the Arrow. The completed Arrows sitting on the flight line (death row) lasted a little longer but finally they too were cut up by welders and trucked away to a scrap dealer from Hamilton, Ontario, under the watchful eyes of Government personnel. The aircraft in final assembly and the various components were likewise destroyed and carted away. The only surviving memory of the Arrow is a hacked off front end of Arrow #206, along with a section of landing gear and two outer wing panels and many controls from the cockpit, such as throttle quadrants, control columns and rudder bars in the National Aviation Museum in Ottawa. The cancellation of the Arrow project not only put an end to the Arrow and the Iroquois engine, but put the kiss of death to one of the most advanced aeronautical research and development organizations in the world. In one fell swoop, a national asset which had been created after years of work came to an abrupt end. It was not just the cancellation of an aircraft, it was the cancellation of an industry. Things like the supersonic transport and double-decked airliners already on the drawing boards went by the wayside. One after another top people were snatched up by our neighbours to the south, who had been waiting on the sidelines with their shopping list of key personnel. Many of these people, giants in their respective fields, moved south; later they helped put man first into space and then onto the moon — they used to live here!

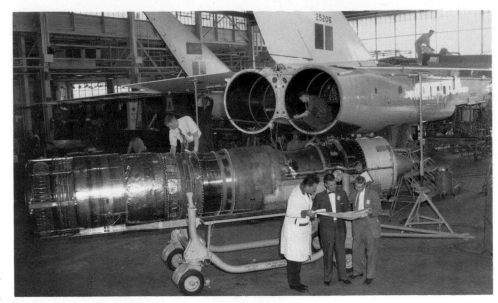

Technicians discussing Iroquois engine installation.

Iroquois engine being readied for installation

Iroquois entering into engine cavity.

Arrow 206 just before Black Friday.

203.   204.   201.   205.   202.

Death Row — five completed Arrows awaiting final outcome.

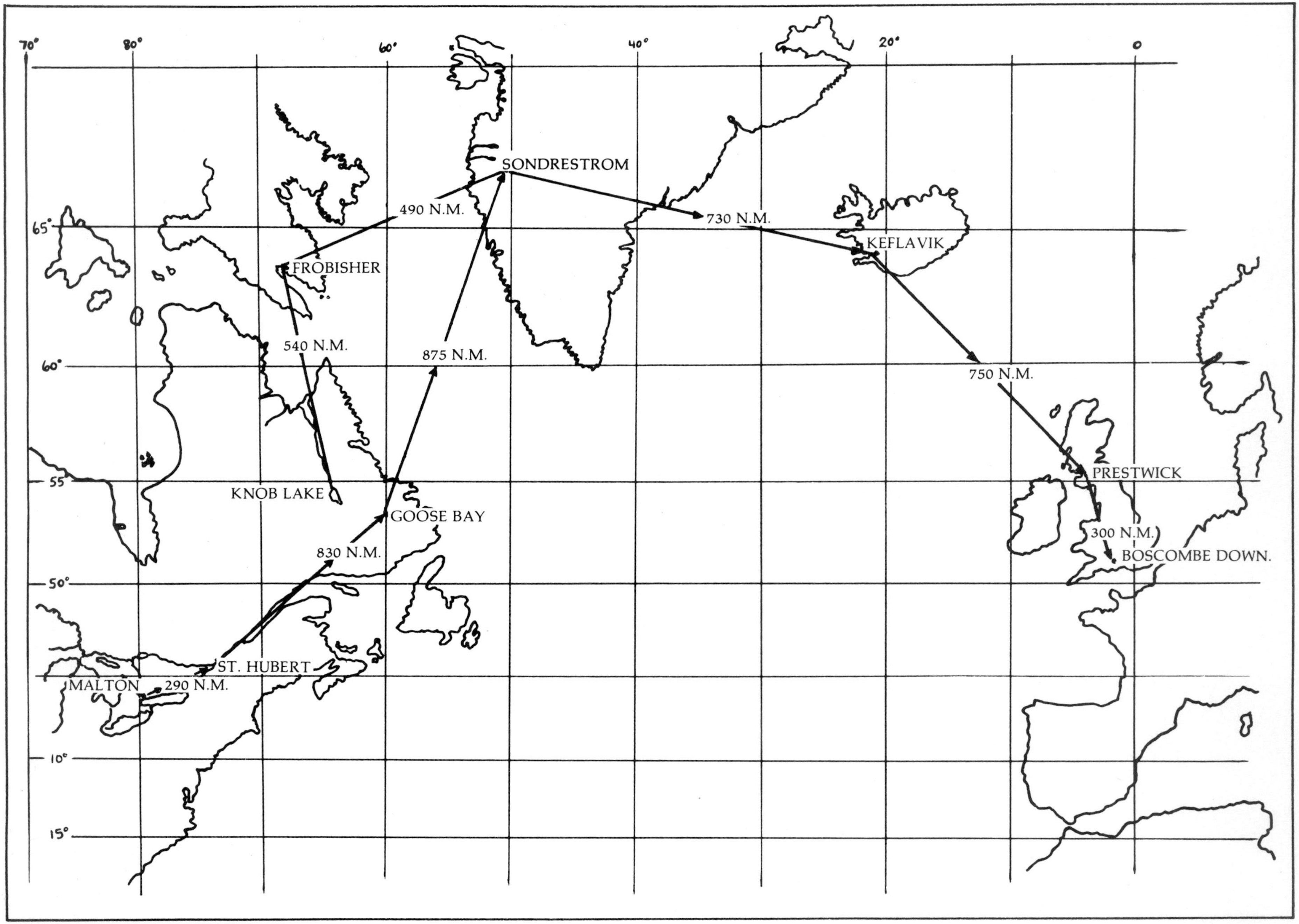

ROUTE FOR PROPOSED FERRY FLIGHT.

BOSCOMBE DOWN.

PRESTWICK

300 N.M.)

750 N.M.

KEFLAVIK

730 N.M.

SONDRESTROM

490 N.M.

875 N.M.

GOOSE BAY

FROBISHER

540 N.M.

830 N.M.

KNOB LAKE

ST. HUBERT

MALTON 290 N.M.

0

20°

40°

60°

80°

70°

65°

60°

55°

50°

10°

15°

The Last Reprieve (almost)
Use of the Arrow 1 for Research on a Supersonic Transport

Following the cancellation of the Arrow Program on February 20th, 1959, a further decision was made to dispose of all aircraft, spares, etc. Five Arrow 1 aircraft with Pratt and Whitney J-75 engines installed, had already flown a total of 70 hours 30 minutes. One virtually completed Arrow 2 aircraft, partly fitted with Iroquois engines, was almost ready to fly, and other Arrow 2's in various stages of final assembly were available.

General Electric announced that they would like to use the Arrows and were prepared to pay a substantial price for them, including purchase of spares, in a straight commercial deal, but the Canadian Government turned them down.

Avro suggested that in view of the proposed program in the United Kingdom, for the design and development of a Mach 2 Supersonic Transport, three Arrow 1's, which had been flying for some time, might be sold as research aircraft to be used in the U.K. program, at a nominal cost; since they were to be disposed of in any event. These aircraft could be used for investigating power plants, systems, equipment, and low and high speed aerodynamics. The aircraft suggested for transfer were numbers 201, 203, and 204.

The main advantage in this approach, apart from the nominal cost, was the fact that they were available immediately and, since time was obviously of the essence on the Mach 2 transport program, research required to provide design answers could be undertaken very early in the program. Two Arrows could be used in various test programs, with the third being held as a spare. It was believed that they would be able to save a great amount of money and thus speed up the development time of the Anglo-Franco aircraft that became "The Concorde".

The Arrows with a complete breakdown of costs including spare parts was prepared and even a route was proposed on how to fly the Arrows from Malton, Canada, to Boscombe Down in Southern England.

The following was the proposed route for ferrying the Arrows from Malton to Boscombe Down:

Malton — St. Hubert	290 N.M.
St. Hubert — Goose	830 N.M.
Goose — Sondrestrom	875 N.M.
(USAF base in Greenland)	
Sondrestrom — Keflavik	730 N.M.
Keflavik — Prestwick	750 N.M.
Prestwick — Boscombe	300 N.M.
Total distance	3775 N.M.

The U.K. approached the Canadian Government about acquiring the Arrows. They were told not to pursue the matter, for if they did, the Canadian Government would be in the embarrassing position of having to say an official "No!"...no Arrows would ever leave Canada!

A short time later all the Arrows were scrapped.

People have often wondered why the Arrow was never continued by the British Avro Co. after cancellation. There are a number of reasons, the most obvious being that it was completely a Canadian Government project. The other reason was that the Canadian requirements were so completely different. In the U.K. the airfields are close together and therefore do not require long range aircraft interceptors. In Canada the reverse was true, especially the distance between airfields in northern Canada. This made it necessary to build a twin engine aircraft for safety and also one with fairly good range, while in the U.K. single engine, short range interceptors were acceptable. The Arrow was built to an RCAF specification, to suit Canadian conditions, which it met and surpassed. The British were interested but for research not for use.

Aerial view discloses destruction of Arrows.

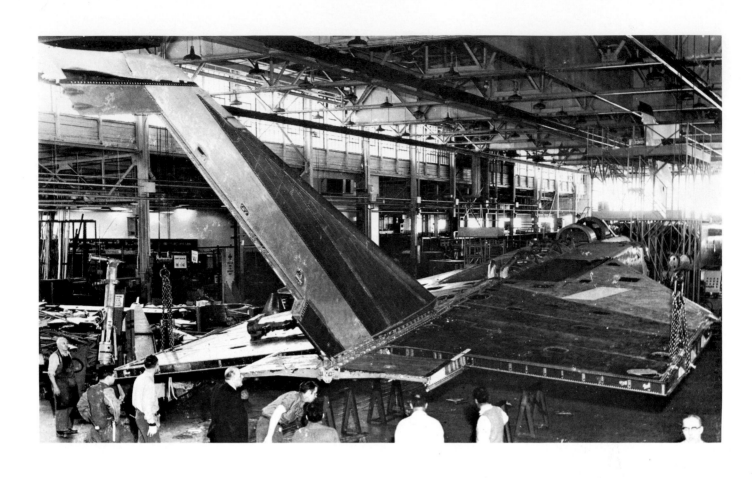

Destruction of Arrows inside Plant.

All that survived the destruction, on display at the Science Museum in Ottawa.

Flight Lieutenant Jack Woodman and Jan Zurakowski are seen at the 50th Anniversary of Powered Flight in Canada (Feb. 23, 1909-1959) display at the 1958 C.N.E. Sadly the Arrow program was terminated just three days short of this great occasion.

Peter Cope (left) and Zura (right) talk about the Arrow with Don Rogers, Manager of Flight Test.

Avro Arrow Summary
for 1959

On February 20th, 1959, the ARROW and IROQUOIS Programs were terminated. For historical record, a summary of operations of the Company for January and February are briefly set forth.

Engineering Division
Arrow 1 and 2 Program

Arrow program expenditure during January was 94% of estimated budget and this increased to 97% during February. Approximately 30% of Arrow manpower was applied to work on the Hughes MA-1 and MB-1 Fire control systems connected with the Falcon weapon program.

All Hughes interim pack structure drawings, and 80% of the Falcon interim pack drawings had been released to the experimental department. Over 20% of production pack drawings had already been released to the manufacturing division. Wind tunnel tests on Hughes MB-1 and Falcon trajectories had been planned, and were scheduled to begin by the end of March 1959.

Work on the flying control was proceeding and consideration was being given by the RCAF to using the ARROW metal mock-up as a training unit.

The Hughes MA-1 fire control electronic system installation was in an advanced stage of design, with flight testing scheduled for mid-May 1959 in aircraft RL 25202.

Design work was continuing on the tie-in of the automatic flight control system with the damper system. AFCS equipment had been checked out with the analogue computer and was being connected to the flight simulator.

A revised performance estimate was prepared, quoting so-called 'guaranteed performance'. This was based on the latest flight test and engine data and appropriate presentation slides were being prepared. The Arrow operational specification was also completed.

Ground Testing

Pre-installation tests were being conducted on aircraft 25206. Out of 41 items to be tested, 31 had been received, 23 tests completed and 8 items were on test.

Development testing continued of Arrow 2's fuel, landing gear and flying control systems. Preliminary test, on strain gauge installations for elevator supersonic loading tests, had been conducted on the static test aircraft and the actual tests had been scheduled to begin on March 2nd, 1959.

Flight Testing

Up to February 20th, 1959, 66 flights had been completed, totalling 70 hours, 30 minutes flying time. Of this amount 7 hours 51 minutes was flown at supersonic speeds.

Aircraft RL25201 made 8 flights for a total of 8 hours 5 minutes during 1959. On its last flight February 19th, 1959, the flight envelope was extended to 550 knots EAS at 35,000 ft. (Mach 1.75).

RL25202 did not fly in 1959.

Aircraft RL25203 flew 3 times in 1959 with 3 hours 20 minutes time. On its last flight of 1 hour 10 minutes February 19th, an observer (D.E. Darrah) was carried and damper optimization was checked.

Arrow RL25204 was airborne 3 flights for a total of 3 hours 35 minutes during 1959. Instrumentation required for RCAF evaluation of the Arrow had been installed and flight tested in this aircraft.

Aircraft RL25205 had flown only on its 40 minute maiden flight on January 11th, 1959, and then been grounded to prepare for landing gear energy absorption and drag chute loading tests. Its next check flight was scheduled for February 21st, 1959.

Arrow Programme		Arrow 1 — 5 Aircraft		
Final Assembly flow				
Aircraft	In Jig	Out Jig	Complete	RCAF Acceptance
25201	June 26/57	July 31/57	Oct. 4/57	Mar. 25/58
25202	Nov. 29/57	Jan. 23/58	Apr. 14/58	June 25/58
25203	Feb. 3/58	Mar. 7/58	May 30/58	Sept. 22/58
25204	Mar. 17/58	Apr. 15/58	July 11/58	Oct. 27/58
25205	Apr. 15/58	May 30/58	Dec. 10/58	Jan. 11/59

A/C 25201

After first flight, the aircraft was turned over to Experimental Division for development purposes. On June 11th, 1958, the aircraft was damaged while landing, repairs were completed by Repair and Overhaul Division. The aircraft next flew again on October 5th, 1958, and was once again engaged in development flying.

A/C 25202

Aircraft accepted by RCAF without first flight. This aircraft was also damaged during development flying with a landing accident November 11th, 1958. The aircraft was under repair in hangar D2 and completion was expected to be the end of February 1959. The right hand outer wing had been repaired by Manufacturing Division and delivered to the aircraft on February 13th, 1959.

Installation of the Hughes XMA-1c fire control system in this aircraft was progressing satisfactorily. The major structure sub-assemblies had been installed and the electrical wiring was also being installed. There were no delays due to shortages of parts from Hughes. It was expected that all would be ready for installation of tested units from Hughes Aircraft due March 20th and that the aircraft would be ready to fly by the end of March 1959.

Arrow 204 in high flight.

Arrow Programme Arrow 2			
Final Assembly Flow			
Aircraft	In Jig	Out Jig	Complete
25206	July 30/58	Oct. 10/58	98%
25207	Oct. 16/58	Nov. 14/58	85%
25208	Nov. 28/58	Jan. 7/59	80%
25209	Jan. 16/59	Feb. 13/59	57%
25210	Feb. 13/59	—	46%

A/C 25206
At cancellation two Iroquois engines were being fitted into the aircraft. Completion had been scheduled for February 20th, 1959. RCAF acceptance due March 1959.

A/C 25207
Completion expected in March 1959. Scheduled RCAF acceptance date May 1959.

A/C 25208
Completion expected April 1959. Scheduled RC-AF acceptance date July 1959.

Component assembly was 91% complete for aircraft 25209.
Component assembly was 8% complete for aircraft up to 25212.
Major components were in work for aircraft up to 25216.
Minor sub components were in work for aircraft up to 25221.

Arrow 2 - 29 Aircraft		
Manufacture of the 43,125 detail parts and the 9,199 sub assemblied as of mid-February 1959 was:		
	Details Complete	Sub-Assemblies Complete
Batch 87—(15 A/C):	34258 (79% of Total Pts.)	6625 (82% of Total Pts.)
Batch 88—(14 A/C):	23735 (55% of Total Pts.)	497 (5% of Total Pts.)

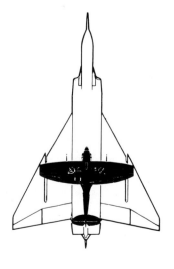

The Arrow was not a small aircraft. The size of aircraft had increased significantly since World War 2. In this silhouette of the Arrow we see a superimposed scaled silhouette of the Clipped-Wing Spitfire Vb.
The length of the Arrow was greater than that of the Avro Lancaster, produced at Malton during the War.

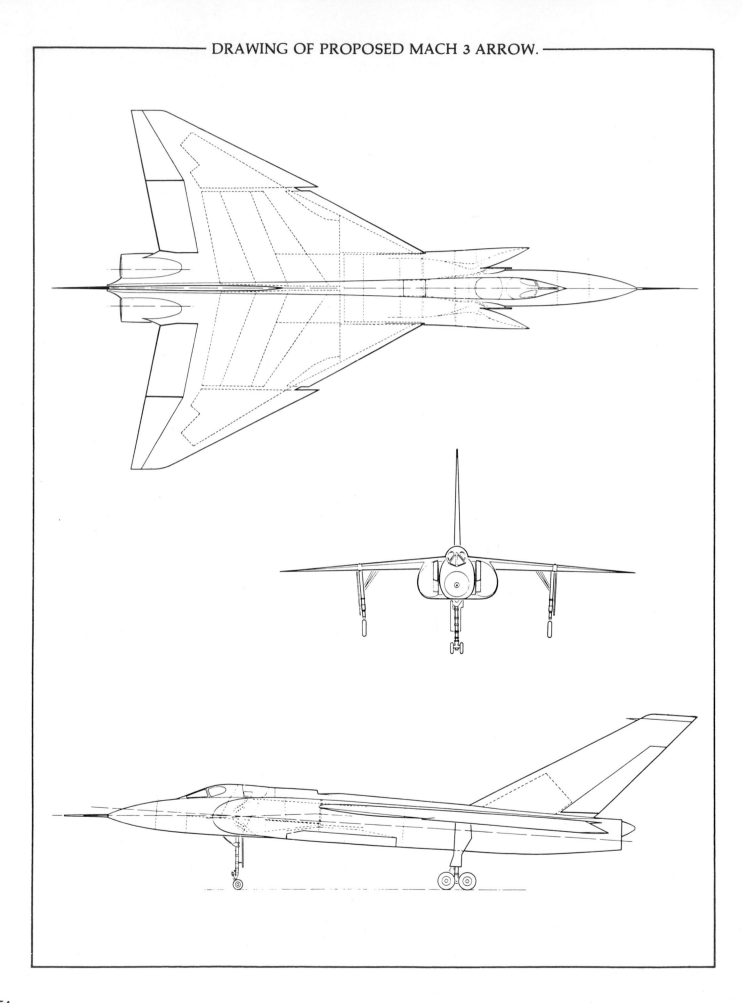

Arrows for the Future

Some might argue the inclusion of a chapter on future proposals for the Arrow, since none were actually built, but we feel that it is most important. The Arrow as built more than met the original specifications (AIR 7-3) as set down by the Air Force. This specification was 200 nautical miles radius and 5 minutes combat at Mach 1.5, but the company (Avro) was always conscious of the fact that if there was a chance of selling the Arrow on an international basis, to the U.K. or the Americans, it would have to give it more range, over and above whatever the RCAF wanted. A number of other projects were also under consideration to improve the aircraft.

It is not fair to say an aircraft is obsolete as soon as it flies, but there is some truth to this and one cannot sit back and say that an aircraft is good in a certain configuration for the next ten or fifteen years. There is always room for improvement! Several Arrow versions were already in preparation by the Project Research Group and in the Initial Projects Office before the Arrow 2 was scheduled to fly.

Here are some of the versions which looked interesting:

Arrow 2A — Increase in Radius of the Arrow to Approximately 650 Nautical Miles Subsonic

The company had been asked unofficially by the RCAF to consider increasing the range of the Arrow 2 beyond its specifications. This would require sufficient internal fuel in the aircraft in its present configuration to fly 600-650 nautical miles and carry out a typical mission of 5 minutes combat at Mach 1.5 at 50,000 feet pulling 2G. Additional fuel would be carried in the fin and wherever else possible. It might be added, that there was nothing new in the technology of putting fuel in the fin, apart from changes to the

centre of gravity (C of G); it's no different from putting fuel in the wings. All this was quite practical and could have been done at very reasonable costs. The study work on this project had been carried out and all the Company needed was a go ahead from the RCAF on the design changes for the Arrow 2A.

Arrow 3 — Increase in Speed to Mach 2.5 in addition to Increase in Internal Fuel as in Arrow 2A

The RCAF had not established a requirement for increased speed but the Company had already carried out a study. Arrow 3 was the same airplane as Arrow 2A with an increase in speed. On a cursory examination, it appeared that the speed could be increased to Mach 2.5. The idea was to replace the fixed engine intakes on the aircraft with variable intakes. This would give reasonable air entry conditions to the engines up to Mach 2.5. There would also be a change in the jet engine nozzle and certain other parts of the aircraft and equipment in order to withstand the higher temperature created. It was estimated that a radius of action of approximately 420 nautical miles (n.m.) could be achieved for supersonic missions and around 500 n.m. subsonic, with supersonic combat of short duration. Combat altitude in both the Arrow 2A and the Arrow 3, with the Iroquois, would go up to about 65,000 feet, which was absoutely phenomenal then and still is. No further work was carried out on this version as the RCAF had not yet shown an interest in increased speed.

Arrow 3A — Increase in Fire Control System Acquisition Range

To exploit the weapon capability of the Arrow 3 Mach 2.5 aircraft, the radar capabilities in the fire control system would have to be improve considerably, because of much higher closing speeds; the Arrow therefore had to see the target much earlier. A study of the latest radar developments would need to be investigated. The Arrow 3A was really an Arrow 3 with better radar, having a longer acquisition range. AVRO waited for the RCAF to establish the requirement.

Reconnaissance Version of the Arrow

A reconnaissance version of the aircraft was investigated. It was thought that a higher supersonic performance could be achieved without sacrifice of subsonic capability, by the utilization of a mixed power plant, of turbojet plus ramjet. Applying this principle to the Arrow, it was thought possible to obtain Mach 2.5 at 90,000 feet. An increase in range could be obtained by carrying extra fuel in an increased outer wing and the use of ramjets in the early stages of flight. A study was also made of the various advantages and disadvantages of a canard Arrow and the substitution of construction materials. The take-off weight of the Reconnaissance Arrow was estimated at about 105,000 lbs. with a range potential of more than 2,000 nautical miles using JP-4 fuel. At the time (July 1957) various means were being worked out to show the exact capability of the Reconnaissance Arrow, A model of the proposed Reconnaissance Arrow was made, A cursory look into high energy fuels indicated that a range increase of possibly 50% might be obtained by direct substitution of high energy fuel for JP-4. The investigation of other high energy fuels was also being monitored. The first practical use of high energy fuel appeared to be in the engine afterburner, since the afterburner pipe could be maintained at a high temperature and thus prevent the deposit of boron sludge. This reconnaissance version of the Arrow was *tentatively called Arrow 4* although never officially so.

Study of Anti-ICBM Missile for the Arrow

For some time AVRO considered the possibility of carrying an anti-missile missile on the Arrow. This would provide a mobile launching platform, giving better weapon mobility, and dispersion.

Trainer Version of the Arrow

Design studies of a dual control trainer version of the Arrow were carried out in anticipation of

future discussion with the Canadian Air Force Training Command.

Intermediate Bomber Version of the Arrow

A proposal was sent to the Royal Air Force (R.A.F.) for their consideration to use the Arrow as a tactical bomber using a stand-off bomb. A standard Arrow 2 could be used with very minimum modification. A ½ scale "Blue Steel" stand-off bomb would be used with a 700 lb. atomic warhead; this was expected to get the required lethality, at a stand-off range of 250 nautical miles. This could be achieved within the 6,000 lb. weapon allowance, especially if ramjets were used to obtain the desired range. Weapons could be launched from the Arrow supersonically. Two missions were proposed —

Case One — included new external wing tanks, each carrying close to 1,000 gallons of fuel. These could be jettisoned when empty. This would provide a mission radius of 750 nautical miles, with allowances on mission profile, the last 150 nautical miles (there and back) being at Mach 2. The stand-off bomb would be released at Mach 2, and would add a further 250 n.m. to the radius, enabling a good sized nuclear warhead to be delivered at a distance of 1,000 n.m. The theoretical mission also included an allowance of 2 minutes for manoeuvering after release of the weapon.

Case 2 — The mission profile is identical to that in Case One, except that this mission uses only internal fuel, extra tanks being added in the outer wing and the bomb bay. The standard external under-fuselage ventral tank is also used and jettisoned when empty. The mission would provide a radius of 635 n.m. to bomb release at Mach 2, or a total, with stand-off bomb of 885 n.m. — Case Two then looks particularly promising, since there would be no major modifications required to the aircraft, the mods being confined to additional internal fuel, and modifications required to electronic equipment items for the tactical role.

The English were not the only ones interested in the Arrow as a bomber. General Kamnhuber, the German Chief of Air Staff, and his senior officers on a visit to AVRO in 1957 mentioned to Air Marshal Slemon that they were most impressed with the Arrow because of its versatility and possible use as a light bomber. They wanted to be kept informed as development progressed.

Also in 1957 Dr. Courtland Perkins, Chief Scientist USAF visited Avro to have a look at the Arrow. He mentioned that the USAF had let out a contract for a design study on a Long Range Interceptor (L.R.I.). This study was being conducted by North American Aviation and included a complete major weapons system, fire control system and engine. The USAF approach had been very similar to that of the RCAF in relation to Arrow. However, he mentioned that in view of the figures coming out of this design study, both in aircraft weight, which was around 110,000 lbs. and the situation on defence dollars, it looked like the project might be discarded in the not too distant future. He felt that because of the timing in the USAF project, there could be an interim aircraft such as the McDonnell F-4H *or the Arrow.*

He went on to say that the Arrow came closer to their requirements than anything they had seen at that time and felt that Avro should keep the USAF constantly aware of the Arrow's progress so that in the event of a cancellation of their L.R.I., there would be a good chance that they would become vitally interested in the Arrow.

The Ultimate Arrow

It is very interesting to note that in the late 50's, the Defence Research Board had carried out a study on the defence of Canada from 1960 to 1970 and it showed a definite requirement for a manned interceptor in addition to guided missiles.

The report favoured the idea of taking the battle north and intercepting the threat as far north as possible primarily because of the hazards of exploding atomic warheads or defensive weapons close to populated areas, and at the same time, to accomplish an interception prior to the point at which the enemy could launch a guided bomb, which might have a range of 200 to 300 miles under its own power, and be difficult to intercept because of speed.

It was indicated that a minimum radius should be considered around 800 miles and that 1,500 was desirable, but that the Air Force should aim for 1,000 nautical miles.

The interceptor should be capable of Mach 3 for at least short bursts, in order to have some pursuit capability over the supersonic bomber threat. This was made increasingly necessary because of the fantastic high closing rates of a supersonic fighter to a supersonic bomber in head-on collision course. It is almost impossible to get sufficient acquisition range to make an attack of this kind when considering the differential in speed of approximately Mach 5. For the same reason a two man crew would probably be required. It was realized that this would be a very large airplane.

The picture on weapons, as usual, was anything but clear in 1959, but that the optimization of aircraft weapons, and fire control systems would require much longer range weapons with larger engines and atomic warheads, with the weapons taking over the manoeuvering phases after launch and allowing some degradation in aircraft manoeuverability.

The general picture, out of this survey, is as follows:

Range: As close to 1,000 miles as possible

Speed: Mach 3 for as long as possible (depending on achieving a practical aircraft weight and runway length).

Altitude: Around 60,000 feet (it was anticipated that the weapon would climb 15 to 20,000 feet above this altitude).

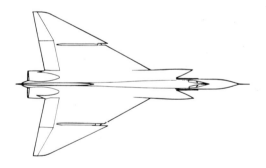

Enter the Arrow Mach 3, still not built but in the planning stage. *This is 1959, before Black Friday.* This new Arrow would have variable engine intakes, modified skin sections and the further developed Iroquois engine, thus extending the state of the art a step further. The ultimate Arrow would give it maximum range and speed within the basic configuration. Other thoughts were also considered; using wing fuel pods; a new undercarriage retracting between the pods; additional ramjet engine power plants, etc. Further studies for pushing the configuration to the limit included the possibility of a zero length launch. The Defence Research Board had recently expressed interest.

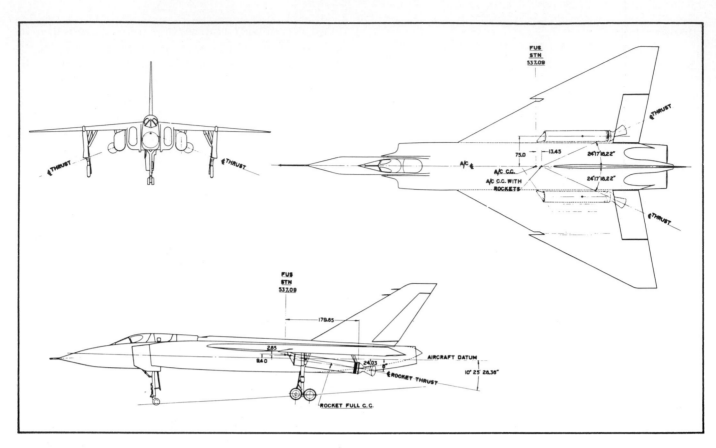

ROCKET GEOMETRY — ZERO LENGTH LAUNCH.

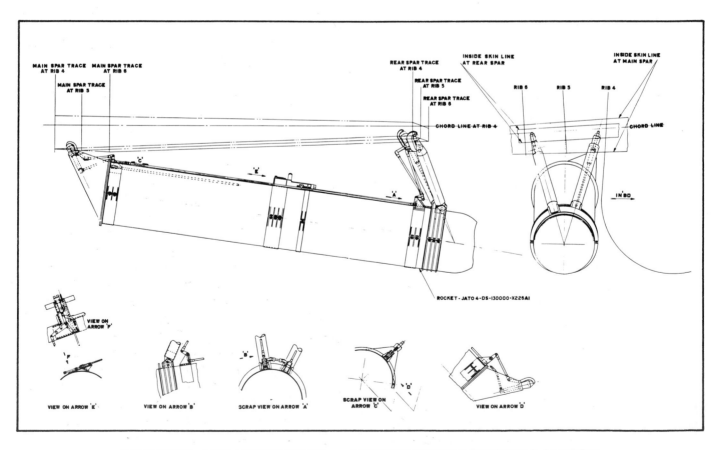

BOOSTER ARRANGEMENT — ARROW ZERO LENGTH LAUNCH.

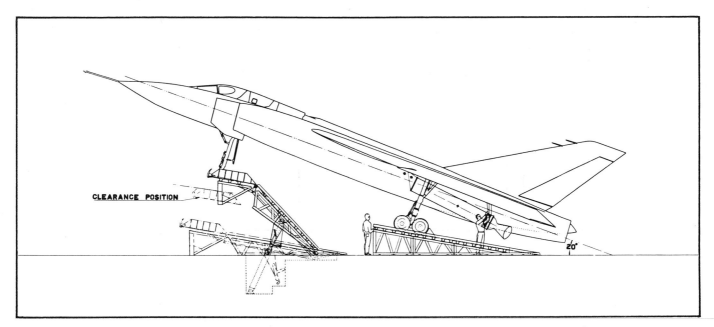

ARROW LAUNCHING POSITION FOR ZERO LENGTH LAUNCH.

Zero Length Launch Arrow (ZELL)

AVRO investigated the feasibility of a zero length launching of the Arrow; a method of launching the Arrow to flying speed without the use of any ground run.

The zero launch operation could be conducted at any location where required and be set up on a 24 hour "at the ready" basis.

In order that the investigation would include possible future developments of the Arrow it was based on the 2A version. This design showed an Aircraft all up weight (A.U.W.) of 76,750 lbs. compared to the A.U.W. of 65,200 lbs. of the Arrow 2. Adding 11,450 lbs. for rocket units and attachments gave a maximum launching weight of 88,200 lbs. estimated.

The zero length launch would require a thrust, in addition to that provided by the engines, sufficient to provide an aircraft trajectory of at least 10 degrees in elevation. This additional thrust would also have to be of sufficient magnitude and duration to ensure flight speed in the shortest possible time consistent with the acceleration tolerances imposed by the airframe and crew.

Examination of the airframe structure revealed that it would be extremely unlikely that a single thrust could be economically applied. It was resolved, therefore, to use two rocket boosters mounted symmetrically to the lower side of the wing. The method adopted consisted of mounting

two JATO TYPE 121 UNITS under the wings with the take-off being accomplished from a ramp supporting the aircraft by means of its undercarriage.

The general configuration of the aircraft, method of mounting the booster units, arrangement of the ramps and method of ejecting the booster are shown on the accompanying drawings.

A trajectory of 10 degrees was considered the minimum to provide clearance for the launch. At the same time a minimum trajectory requires minimum boost thrust and reduces the time to controllable flight speed. Ten degrees was chosen in consideration of these two characteristics.

At the period in the launch at which controllable flight speed is reached, or at the slightly higher speed at which burnout of the boosters occurs, it is desirable that the incidence of the aircraft be at the normal one for that speed. This provides a smooth transition from boosted launch to normal climb and obviates a sudden demand on the pilot to correct for incidence at a time when he would probably be correcting for other deviations.

Combining the trajectory with the incidence gives a 20 degree attitude for the aircraft datum and this applies to the static position on the ramps. The aircraft would be supported on three ramps, one for each undercarriage. Due to the 20 degree datum angle, it would be necessary to raise the main undercarriage above the ground to avoid interference of the rear of the jet pipes with the ground. The aircraft would be winched up onto the ramps, the main wheels locked to prevent roll back, and the nose gear then elevated to give the desired datum angle. The nose wheels would have to be attached to the ramp during elevation because the centre of gravity passes behind the main gear fulcrum point.

Examination of loads and stresses indicated that some modification would be required in the vicinity of the booster attachments to the wing but these did not appear to be of a serious nature.

In an actual launch the pilot would actuate a button or a switch which would fire both boosters simultaneously, all locks between the aircraft and the ramps would be released and the nose gear ramp would be quickly lowered to allow the rear fuselage to clear it on takeoff.

It was assumed that engine thrust would be 44,000 lbs.; each booster was capable of approximately 132,000 lbs. or 308,000 lbs. combined total thrust. This would give an acceleration of 3G.

It was estimated that at 2 seconds from zero the airspeed would be 108 knots and at 3 seconds 165 knots. Up to 2 seconds controls would be ineffective but between 2 to 3 seconds control would increase rapidly. This would allow the pilot to correct any deviation starting at approximately the 2 second point. Duration of the launch would be approximately 3.71 seconds at which time burn-out would occur. After burn-out the rocket boosters could be jettisoned from the aircraft as they would no longer be required.

Although any final design may have differed in geometry, weight etc. from that assumed in this analysis, this gives a representative range of values that were expected.

High Performance Arrow

It was felt by the Project Research Group that if they could obtain encouragement on an aircraft like that of Arrow 4, a greater step should be considered — an airplane of Mach 4 to 5, altitude of 100,000 feet, and an operational radius of 1,000 nautical miles. Although quite a tall order, knowledge gained during the Arrow program might provide a means of accomplishing this.

Most of these studies were worked through to a conclusion and the results submitted to the Design Council. Obviously none of them got any further. The Project Research Group believed in doing something that either the competitors had not already done or something the competitors were already doing, but doing it better to beat them out.

Arrows of the Future — Today and for Tomorrow

In looking back, it would be safe to say that had the Arrow Program not been cancelled and the Iroquois been allowed to be fully developed, there would certainly have been an Arrow flying today, and well into the 1980's.

In this book, we have looked at the Arrow, as it was in 1959. With continued development and modifications who knows what successive Mk's would have brought. History has proven that an advanced all-weather interceptor, with long range supersonic capabilities was needed, and was not replaced by the new missile age. Indeed it looks like the manned interceptor, together with missiles, will be in use in the foreseeable future.

If the Arrow and the Iroquois had been continued, the NATO countries would have had a first rate interceptor and our country's balance of payments may probably have been in a better shape, as our NATO partners lined up to place their orders for the Arrow. Possibly there could have been an Iroquois engine used in the Vietnam War by the U.S. where the MIG-21 demonstrated the need for simpler, more rugged fighters and engines. The Iroquois was noted for its simplicity. With the cancellation of the Arrow, the Iroquois engine met the same fate as the Arrow. Orenda could not complete its licensing agreements until the engine was certified, and since Ottawa clearly had no enthusiasm for the engine, its design and development capability soon diminished into obscurity and with it any hopes for selling the engine abroad. Had growing momentum been allowed to continue, we would have seen many new advances in aviation originating from Canada, a then recognized world leader in research and development. We were at the doorstep of the future and it was Canada's chance to lead the aviation world.

To Quote Jim Floyd:

"The Arrow Mk1 that flew in 1958-59 was only the first of a fine family of aircraft. With normal development, it would have been a most interesting family!"

Now one can only guess as to what could have been!

Epilog

One thing that should be made quite clear. The Arrow was a truly Canadian product by Canadians for Canada. The Arrow and Iroquois programs were a pinnacle of Canadian aviation achievement, the like of which we may never see again. It was a time when the eyes of the Aviation world were on Canada.

The design, construction and development of these two fine products was the Canadian equivalent to putting a man on the Moon.

The tragedy is that although we demonstrated success, we were never able to reap the benefits.

AVRO CF-105
ARROW mk.1

MANUFACTURED BY A.V.ROE CANADA LTD.
MALTON, ONT. 1957-59

SPAN 50 FT. 0 IN.
LENGTH 77 FT. 9.65 IN.
HEIGHT 21 FT. 3 IN.

POWERED BY TWO
PRATT & WHITNEY J75's

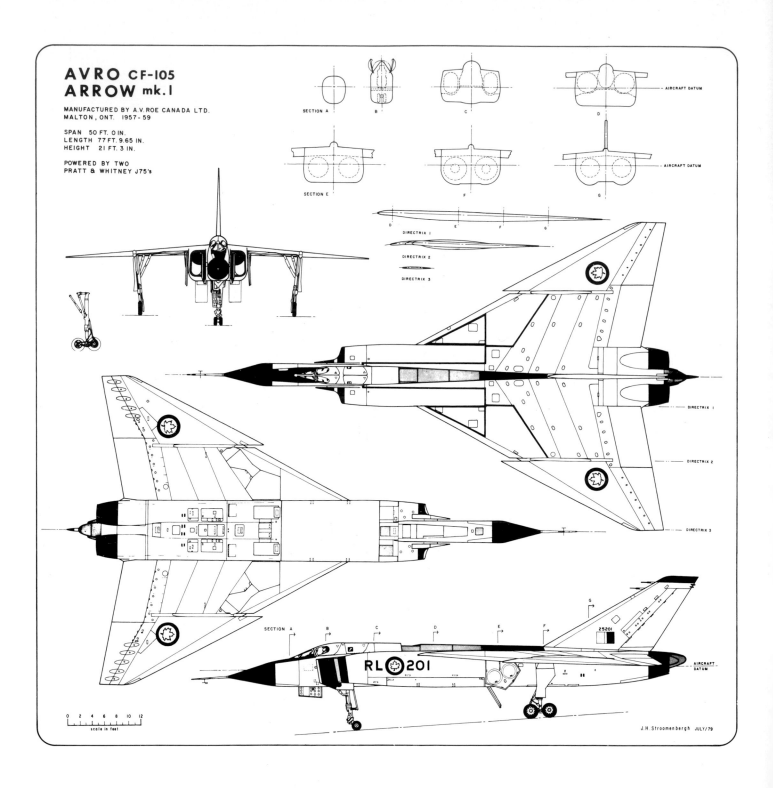

SECTION A
B
C
D — AIRCRAFT DATUM

SECTION E
F
G — AIRCRAFT DATUM

DIRECTRIX 1
DIRECTRIX 2
DIRECTRIX 3

RL○201
25201
AIRCRAFT DATUM

0 2 4 6 8 10 12
scale in feet

J.H. Stroomenbergh JULY/79

162

Technical Data and Drawings

Introduction

To explain in detail the design of the Avro Arrow would require a rather large book or possibly several books. The dedicated technician would like to see recorded, and explained, every one of the many systems and structures contained in this sophisticated and intricate weapon of defence.

The lay reader would be asleep after reading only a few pages of a presentation of this nature. We can only hope, in one short chapter, to provide some idea of the aircraft's size, complexity and structure.

In order to do this, we must recall that old adage of "One Photo Is Worth a Thousand Words." The photos have been seen earlier in the book, with limited explanation in the text. We now present a series of drawings, to give some basic information and details.

Configuration

2 Crew
— complexity of fire control systems
— requirement to perform manual controlled attack in the event of automatic system failure

2 Engines
— dual engine safety
— large weapon payload and fuel load dictated aircraft size too large for any single engine

Fuselage Configuration
— two seats
— large armament bay

Delta Wing
— very thin wing required for supersonic speed
— structural and aeroelastic efficiency of Delta wing made achievement of very thin wing with low thickness/chord ratio possible
— large internal fuel capacity and room for undercarriage

Tailless Configuration
— problem of mounting horizontal tail on very thin fin
— stalling characteristics objectionable with horizontal tail
— tailless Delta information available from Avro in U.K.

Wing Notch and Leading Edge Extension
— to cure anticipated pitch-up problems

Leading Edge Droop
— to increase buffet boundary by preventing leading edge aerodynamic breakaway at high angles of attack

Anhedral (4 degree)
— to reduce landing gear length
— no appreciable aerodynamic effect

High Wing
— lowest structural weight
— straight through wing structure and simple wing/fin attachment
— good access to engines and armament

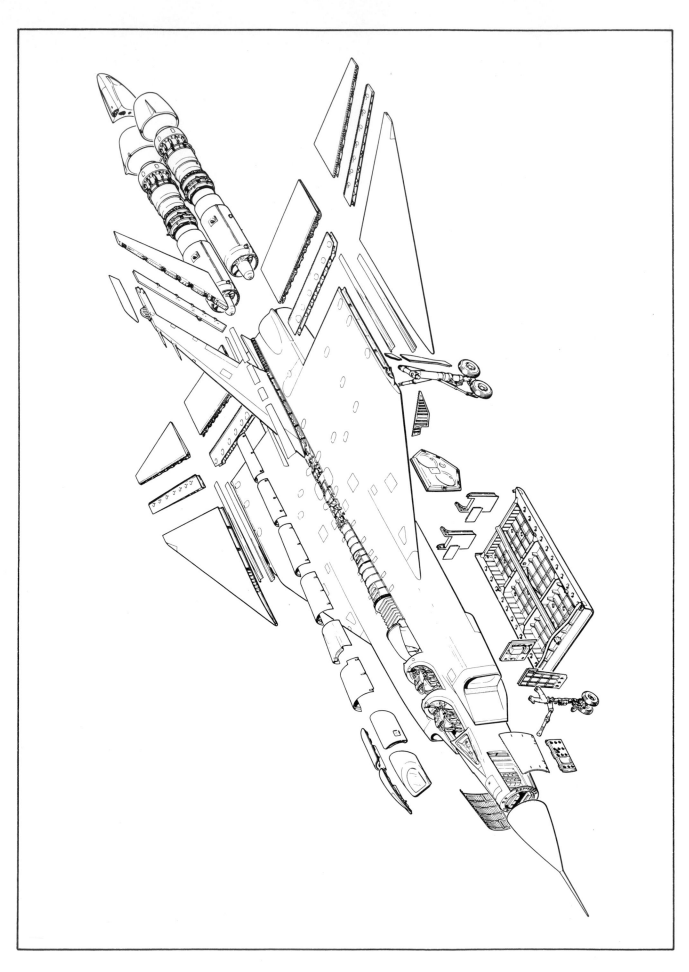

CF-105 (J-75 ENGINE) STRUCTURE CUTAWAY

Area Rule

— from computer data, radar nose sharpened, intake lips thinned, fuselage cross section area reduced below cockpit, extension fairing added at rear

Engine Installation

— Iroquois finally selected for Mk. 2 production and service aircraft

— fixed geometry intake therefore excess ram air to engines at supersonic speed; to eliminate spill and related high drag penalty, gills opened automatically at high speed and allowed excess air to pass over engine, cooling engine and afterburner, then passed into ejector annulus poviding small additional thrust.

Air Intakes

— fixed geometry with boundary layer bleed diverting 2/3 of boundary layer over and under wing, remaining 1/3 to heat exchangers of air conditioning system; intake ramp to create oblique shock wave at supersonic speed and allow optimum pressure recovery inside intake as well as prevent turbulence in intake, over the Mach number range

— perforations of intake ramp to suck off boundary layer air and prevent intake "buzz"

Wings

— high delta wing monoplane aerofoil section NACA 0003.5-6-3.7 Mod. at root with 0003.8-6-3.7 Mod. at tip; inner wing, four spar main torsion box, ribs parallel to fuselage, aluminum alloy machined skins with integral stiffeners (box formed integral fuel tank); outer wings joined to inner by a peripheral bolted joint, multi-spar box beam, machined tapered skins, trailing edge consisted of control boxes housing aileron attached with continuous piano hinge, aileron ribs normal to rear spar.

Fuselage

— aluminum alloy stressed skin construction designed around two engines and associated intakes; fuselage sides attached to wings chordwise by continuous piano hinge, heavy formers attach wing to fuselage; cockpit between intakes; removable armament pack below intakes at centre section; titanium skin in jet pipe area

Empennage

— no horizontal tailplane, large vertical fin and rudder, machined skins

Landing Gear

— tricycle type, nose wheel and strut retracting forward in fuselage, main wheels retracting inward into wings, twisting during retraction. Dual nose wheels, two wheel "tandem bogie" main wheel units track 30'2.5"

Power Plant — Arrow 1

— two Pratt & Whitney J75 P3 (1st a/c) P5 (a/c 2-5) turbojet engines, 12,500 lb. static thrust dry, 18,500 lb. static thrust with afterburning Arrow 2, two Orenda PS-13 Iroquois turbojet engines, 19,250 lb. static thrust dry, 26,000 lb. static thrust with afterburning

Fuel

— two rubber cell type tanks in fuselage, six integral tanks in each wing, total fuel capacity 2897 Imp.Gal., total useable fuel 2508 Imp.Gal., provision of Mk. 2 aircraft for one 500 Imp.Gal. external drop tank. Projected Mk. 2A and Mk. 3 versions with additional internal fuel.

Accommodation

— crew of two, pilot and systems operator in tandem pressurized, air-conditioned cockpits, electrically actuated clamshell canopies with emergency explosive opening devices; Martin Baker C5 ejection seats.

mament

— Mk. 1, no armament, weapons bay occupied with test instrumentation.

— Mk. 2, Hughes Mx1179 fire control and 8 Falcon missiles in enclosed weapons bay. Quickly interchangeable armament pack.

Dimensions

— wing span 50'; length Mk. 1 73'4", 80'10" including probe; Mk. 2 78'. 85'6" including probe; height 21'3"; wing sweepback L.E. 61 degrees 27', T.E. 11 degrees 12'; anhedral 4 degrees; wing area 1225 sq.ft.; root chord at centre line of aircraft 45', tip chord 52.98".

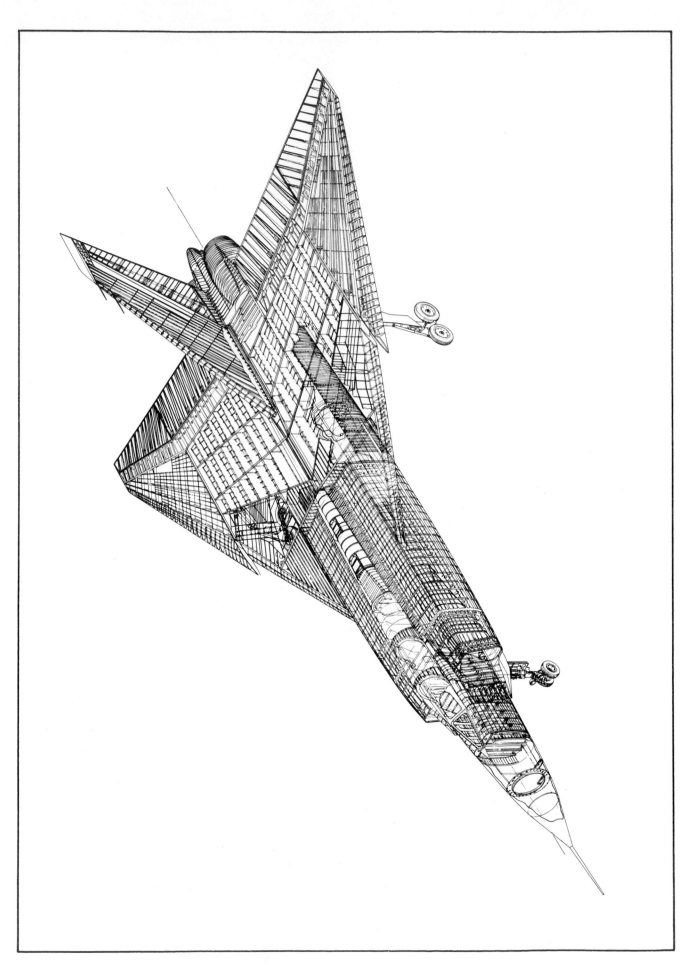

CF-105 (J-75 ENGINE) STRUCTURE CUTAWAY

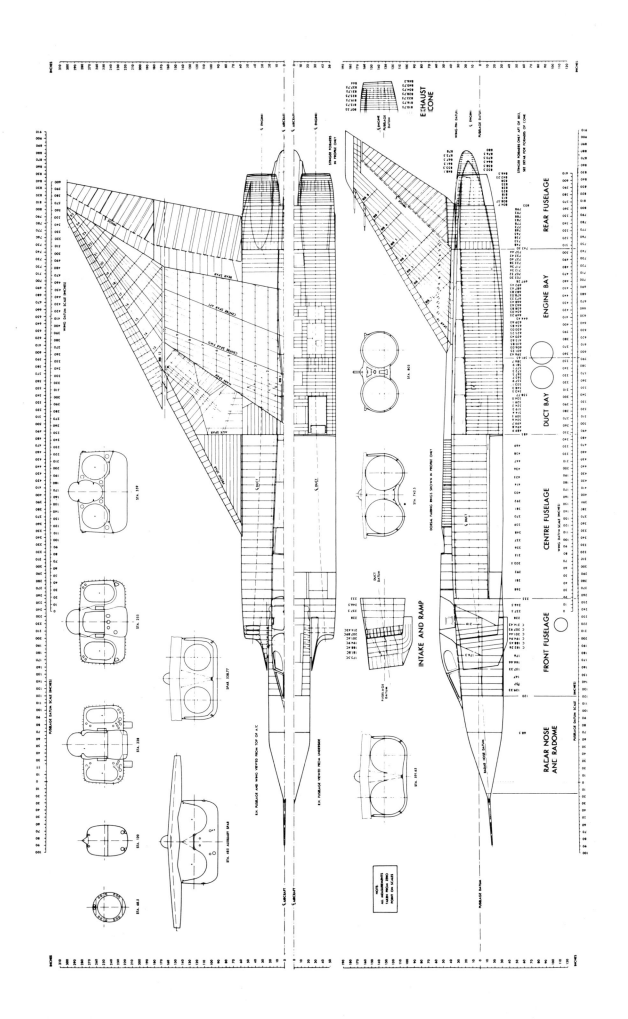

ARROW 1 (J-75 ENGINE) STATION DIAGRAM

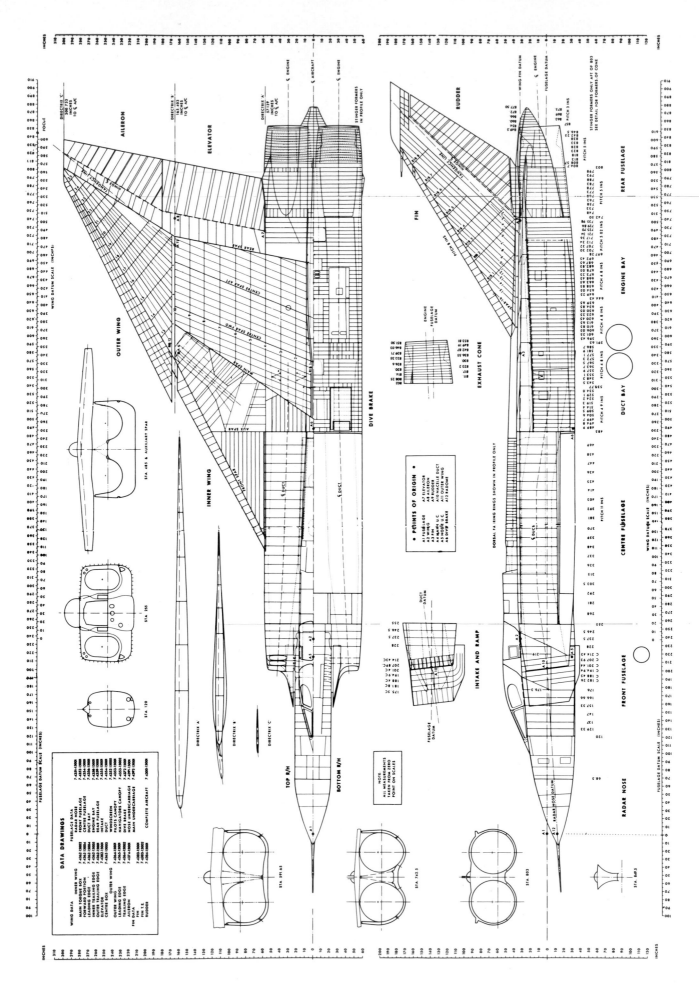

ARROW 2 (IROQUOIS ENGINE) STATION AND DATUM LINES 3 VIEW GENERAL ARRANGEMENT

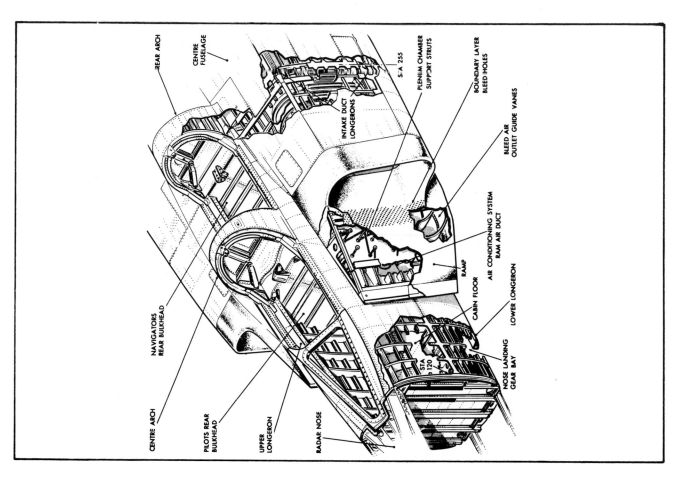

FRONT FUSELAGE

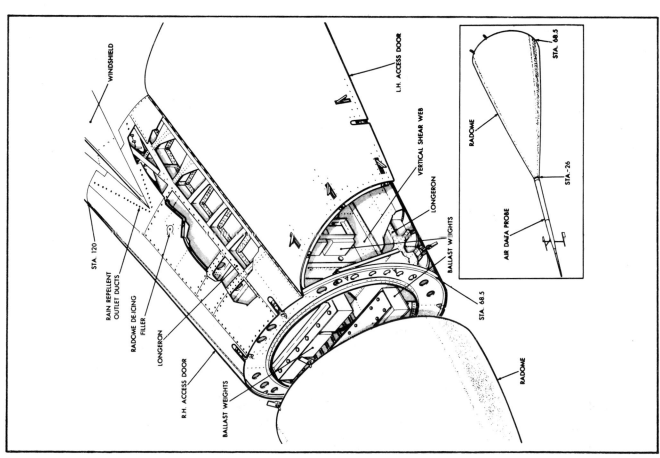

RADAR DOME

169

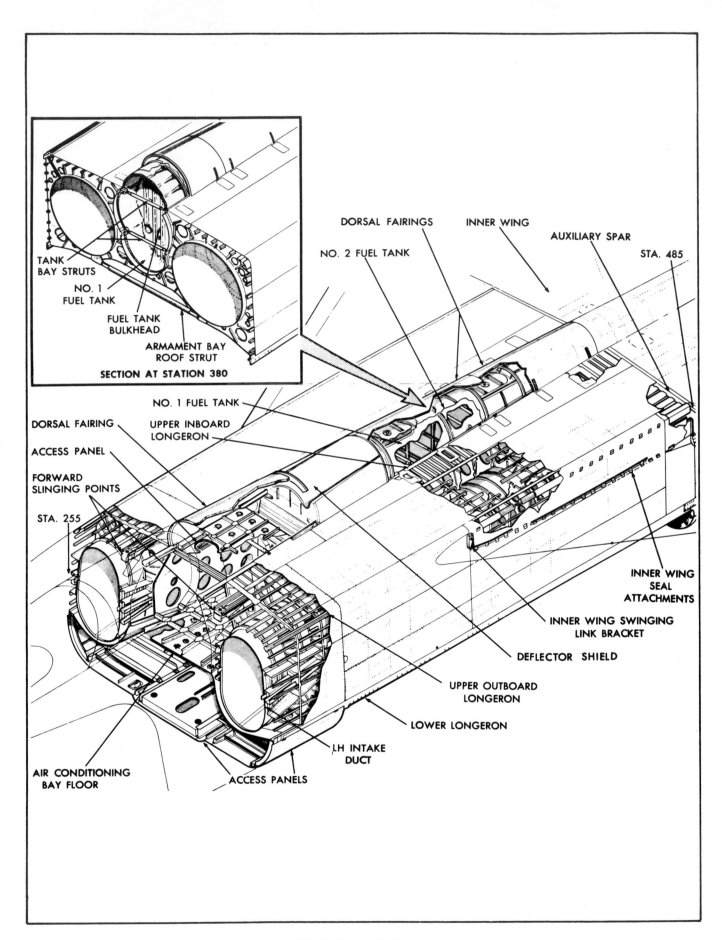

TANK BAY STRUTS

NO. 1 FUEL TANK

FUEL TANK BULKHEAD

ARMAMENT BAY ROOF STRUT

SECTION AT STATION 380

DORSAL FAIRINGS

NO. 2 FUEL TANK

INNER WING

AUXILIARY SPAR

STA. 485

NO. 1 FUEL TANK

UPPER INBOARD LONGERON

DORSAL FAIRING

ACCESS PANEL

FORWARD SLINGING POINTS

STA. 255

INNER WING SEAL ATTACHMENTS

INNER WING SWINGING LINK BRACKET

DEFLECTOR SHIELD

UPPER OUTBOARD LONGERON

LOWER LONGERON

LH INTAKE DUCT

AIR CONDITIONING BAY FLOOR

ACCESS PANELS

CENTRE FUSELAGE

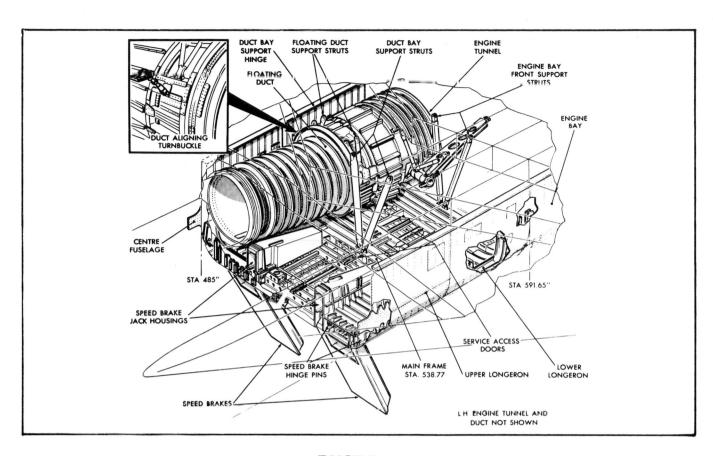

DUCT BAY

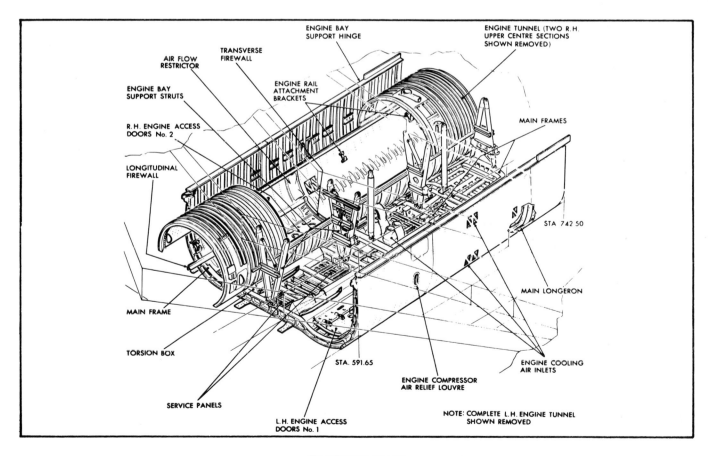

ENGINE BAY

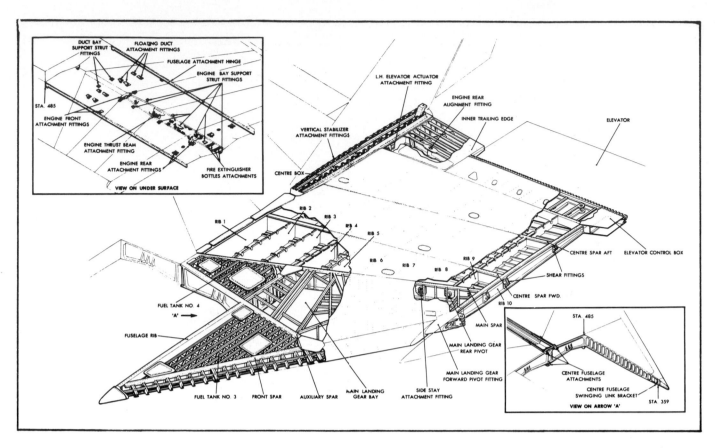

INNER WING

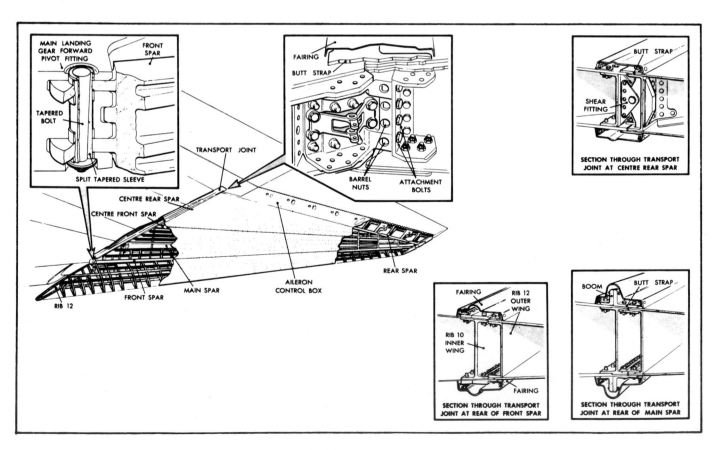

OUTER WING

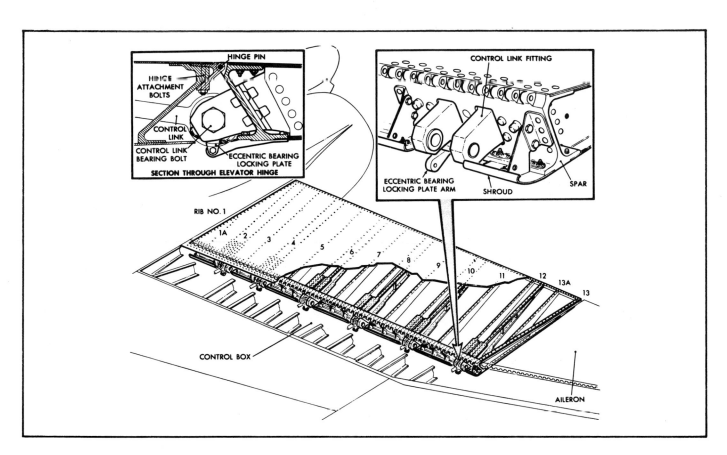

ELEVATOR

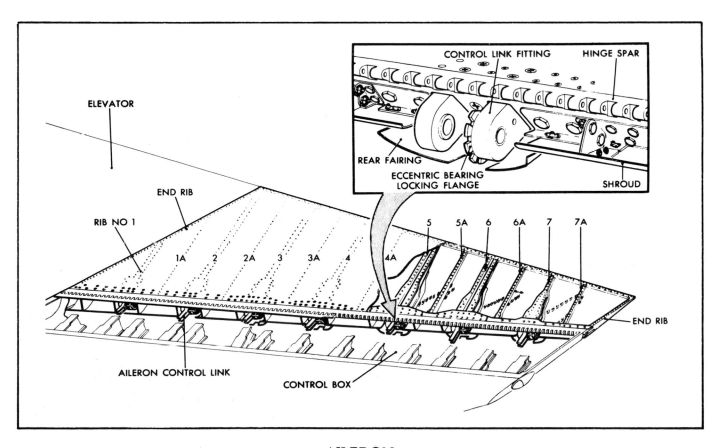

AILERON

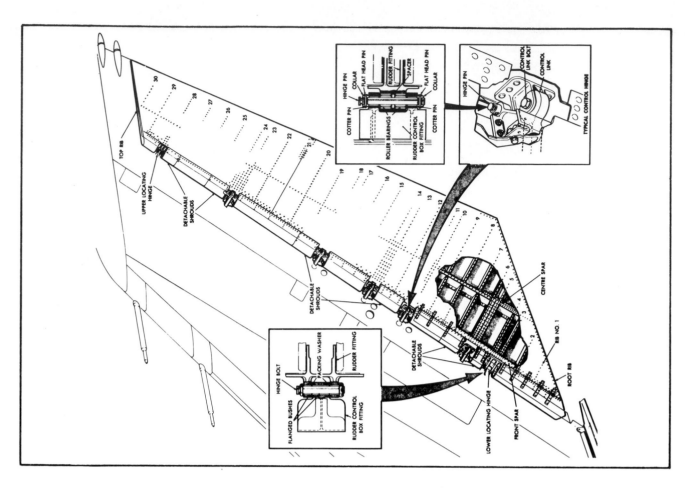

RUDDER

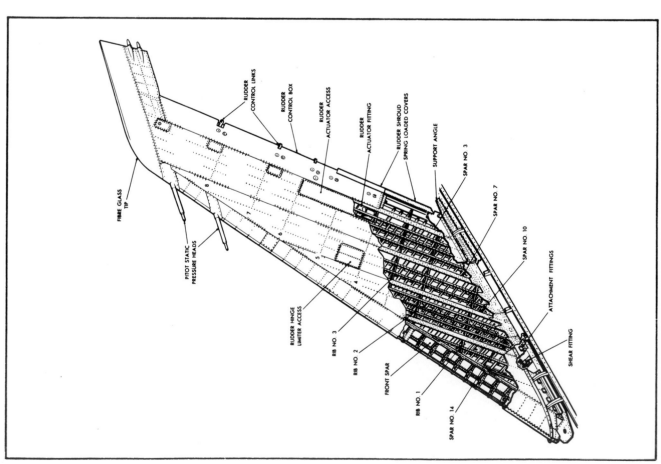

VERTICAL STABILIZER

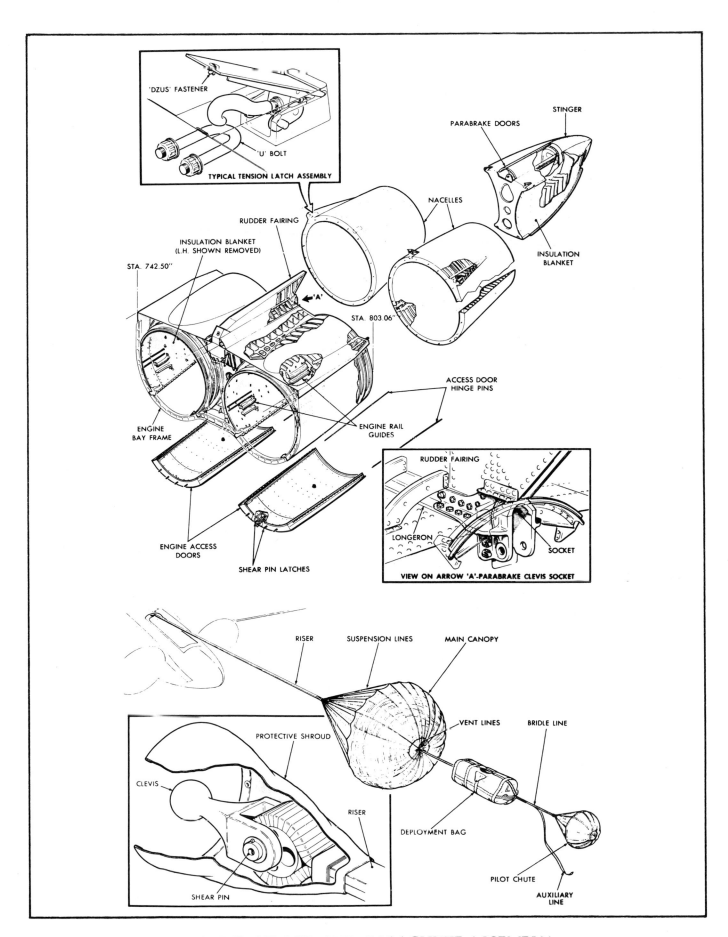

'DZUS' FASTENER

'U' BOLT

TYPICAL TENSION LATCH ASSEMBLY

PARABRAKE DOORS

STINGER

NACELLES

RUDDER FAIRING

INSULATION BLANKET
(L.H. SHOWN REMOVED)

STA. 742.50"

'A'

INSULATION BLANKET

STA. 803.06"

ACCESS DOOR
HINGE PINS

ENGINE
BAY FRAME

ENGINE RAIL
GUIDES

ENGINE ACCESS
DOORS

SHEAR PIN LATCHES

RUDDER FAIRING

LONGERON

SOCKET

VIEW ON ARROW 'A'-PARABRAKE CLEVIS SOCKET

RISER

SUSPENSION LINES

MAIN CANOPY

VENT LINES

BRIDLE LINE

PROTECTIVE SHROUD

CLEVIS

RISER

DEPLOYMENT BAG

SHEAR PIN

PILOT CHUTE

AUXILIARY
LINE

REAR FUSELAGE AND PARACHUTE ASSEMBLY

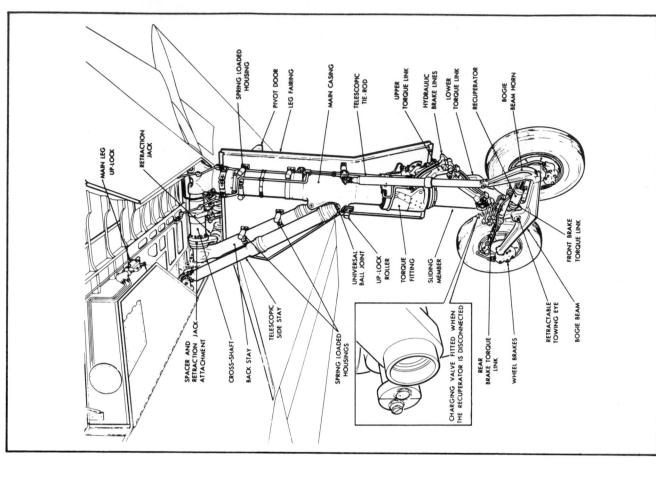

MAIN LANDING GEAR

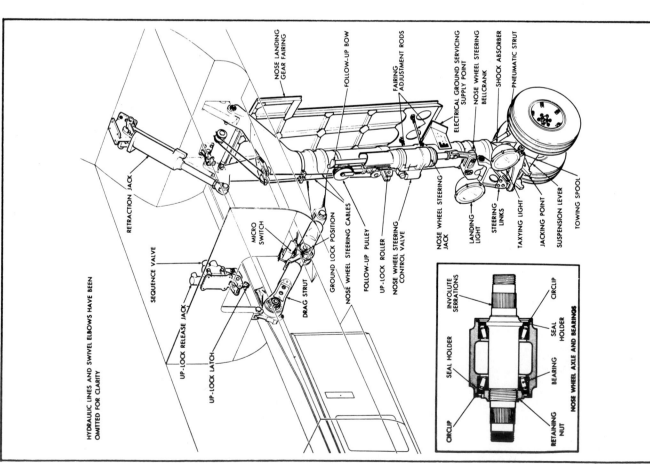

NOSE LANDING GEAR

The Addendum – 30 Years Later

by
R.D. Page

It is 10 years since the Avro Arrow book was published by The Boston Mills Press and 25,000 copies of the book have been printed and sold. This is a phenomenal number of copies of such a technical and expensive book (a best seller in Canada of this type of book would be between 5,000 and 7,000 copies). It is important to record, that this was the publishing house's first all colour hard cover book. The first printing of 2,000 copies sold out in 14 days, and the second printing sold out in 19 days, a month later. This was 21 years after the demise of the Arrow, so it was relatively old news. From there it was a continuous process of printing enough books to meet the constant demand per year. Each year the publisher expected the demand to fall off and each year the orders have come in from far and wide. What was also unique about the event was that there had been a number of good books on the subject which had already been published.

Now more than three decades later, the legend of the Arrow still grows. There is a certain aura surrounding this event in Canadian aviation history, which has formed a cult of Arrow buffs.

The Boston Mills Press has now published three other books associated with the aircraft products of Avro Canada. They are *The Canuck CF-100 All-Weather Fighter* by one of the original Arrowheads, Ron Page; *The Avro Canada C-102 Jetliner* by Jim Floyd, the designer of the Avro Arrow and *Mynarski's Lanc* by Bette Page. All there is left to be done to complete the series on the Avro Canada aircraft is *The Avrocar – Canada's Flying Saucer*. This will be published in some form, in the future.

The Arrow buffs will probably be surprised to learn that the front cover of the *Arrow* book is really a photograph of 201, not 205. The photograph was suitably modified to represent the last Arrow as there were no good air to air shots of it on its one and only flight before it was destroyed with all the other Arrows built and under construction.

There has been a lot of press on the Arrow over the years retelling the story. There have been a number of very large reunions of the old Avro-ites personnel celebrating the various anniversaries of the first flight and cancellation of the Avro Arrow and Orenda Engines Iroquois programmes.

A recent article by Paul Campagna *Avro Arrow – An Aviation Chapter in Canadian History* in the Engineering Dimensions The Official Journal, Association of Professional Engineers of Ontario, on the 30th anniversary of the Arrow produced an amazing response from people who were there. I think it is only appropriate to quote from some of these responses, to remind people what a great technical achievement the Arrow was in so many ways. Also it is important to remove the negative attitude some historians have created in reporting on our history.

The first positive statement is by K.M. Molson who reminds us that the hydraulic system was unique, as "It was the first 4,000 psi system to fly. It was not until some 16 years later that it was followed by another such system in the Rockwell B-1 bomber." This meant that all the actuators, valves, pumps and fittings had to be developed, tested and qualified for flight. Such a high pressure system was necessary to allow the equipment to be smaller and lighter so it could fit into the thin wing of the aircraft.

Jim Floyd, who was Vice-President Engineering, A.V. Roe, Canada, after correcting a number of minor errors in the article, goes on to make the point on Diefenbaker's cancellation of the Arrow. "I mentioned the rising costs, but I also qualified that by saying that Avro's final fixed price of $3.5 million for aircraft, engines and all technical support was the *bargain of the century*. I wish to make that point very firmly." He also reminded the readers in his rebuff to Dr. Desmond Morton for his monumental error concerning the weapon pack, that a derivative of the Hughes Mx1179 fire control system coupled with the Hughes Falcon missiles was the final configuration offered to the RCAF, before cancellation. The Astra-Sparrow combination had been cancelled earlier.

Rodney Rose, ex-Avro, reminds us of the unique drag reduction design of the "the integrated intake/engine bypass/aerodynamic ejector system used on the Arrow – again, well ahead of its time." (see page 122 for a diagram of this system)

Dennis E. Fielder, Flight Test Department, emphasizes "the telemetry system used to bring the flight instrument measurements to the ground control area where the information was available in what today is often called *real time*." This was in the days before the micro-chip, as all the on-board and ground computers were the heavy power-hungry vacuum tube type. The introduction of the micro-chip technology would have been a major performance gain to the aircraft, in weight and space reduction, with the resultant increase in speed and range.

Fielder, Rose and Westall all mention Jim Chamberlin (deceased), who was the aerodynamic brain behind the Arrow, who after the cancellation, joined the NASA space program and became a lead designer on the Apollo program involved in putting *a man on the moon*.

Ross W. Buskard, BGen (retired), who was a member of the RCAF armament test team at the U.S. Naval Missile Test Centre, comments on the weapons system. He says "the decision to abandon the Sparrow was made by the RCAF test team (CEPE ultra west) at Point Mugu, California, not by Avro." It is his opinion that an operational integrated weapons system was at least four years away when the decision to cancel was taken. This length of time for the development and operational trials of such an advanced system was not unusual and even today's armament systems have very long gestation periods.

There were other responses both positive and negative. I, like Jim Floyd, am proud to be Canadian and know that we Canadians can and have produced some of the world's leading engineering projects, such as the St. Lawrence Seaway, the CANDU nuclear power reactor, the Canadarm for the space shuttle and the future space station, are just a few examples. Too many Canadians are willing to believe we are second rate and therefore perpetuate this mentality in our present and future generations.

As this edition was being prepared, two significant events occurred associated with the Arrow story. First, was the publication of Greig Stewart's National Business Award winning book, *Shutting Down The National Dream. A.V. Roe and The Tragedy of The AVRO ARROW*, published by McGraw-Hill Ryerson Ltd., which records the people involved and the circumstances of the rise and fall of A.V. Roe Canada. The second appropriate event for the end of this edition was the organization of *The Aerospace Heritage Foundation of Canada*, whose aim is to build a museum quality full-scale replica of the *Avro Arrow*. It is to be built out of wood and to be used in a film dramatization of the Avro Arrow story by Northlands Film Studio by 1992, after which it will be displayed as a proper museum specimen of Canada's aviation history for all the Canadian public to see. A scale model of the Arrow is used in the play *Avro Arrow* presented by the Canadian Stage Company at the Bluma Appel Theatre of the St. Lawrence Centre for the Arts.

So the *Avro Arrow CF-105* will rise like the phoenix, out of the mass destruction ashes of the past and be a symbol of Canada's aviation history.

National Aviation Museum in Ottawa.

Bibliography

Dow, James, *The Arrow*, James Lormier & Co., Publishers, Toronto, 1979.

Campagna, Paul, AVRO ARROW – An Aviation Chapter in Canadian History, *Engineering Dimensions Journal*, September/October 1988, Vol. 9, No. 5, pp. 46-53.

Engineering Dimensions Journal, K.M. Molson, Avro Arrow: Another Chapter Vol. 9, No. 6, pp. 6, November/December 1988.

Engineering Dimensions Journal, Bringing Down the Arrow: A 30-Year Retrospective, Many contributors, Vol. 10, No. 1, pp. 33 - 36, pp. 55. January/February 1989.

Floyd, James C., "The Canadian Approach to All-Weather Interceptor Development." *Journal of the Royal Aeronautical Society, Vol. 62, No. 576, December 1958.*

———. *"The Avro Canada Story." Canada Aviation,* June 1978.

———. *The Avro Canada C. 102 Jetliner.* The Boston Mills Press, Erin, Ontario, 1986.

Gunston, Bill, *Early Supersonic Fighters of the West,* Shepperton, Surrey: Ian Allen Ltd., 1976.

Molson, K.M. & Taylor, H.A. *Canadian Aircraft since 1909,* Canada's Wings, Inc. 1982.

Pedden, Murray, *Fall Of An Arrow,* Stoddart Publishing, 1987. (First published by Canada's Wings, Stittsville, Ontario, 1979.)

Shaw, Kate E., *There Never was an Arrow,* Steel Rail Publishing, Toronto, 1979, 1981.

Stewart, Greig, *Shutting Down The National Dream, A.V. Roe and The Tragedy of The AVRO ARROW,* McGraw-Hill Ryerson Ltd., Scarborough, Ontario, 1988.

Index

Avery, B.A. (Burt) 123
Buskard, BGen Ross W. (retired) 164
Campagna, Paul 163, 179
Chamberlin, Jim 35, 164
Cook-Craigie 21
Cooper-Slipper, Mike 127, 131
Cope, Peter 72, 77, 112, 116, 119, 150
Darrah, D.E. (Red) 88, 89, 114
Dow, James 179
Fielder, Dennis E. 164
Floyd, J.C. (Jim) 35, 49, 160, 163, 164, 179
Foottit, W/C R. 13
Gordon, Crawford 141
Grinyer, Charles A. 123
Gunston, Bill 133, 179
Hake, Guest 35
Hobbs, Len 127
Kamnhuber, General 156
Keast, F.H. (Harry) 123
Kwiatkowski, Stan 48
Lindley, R.N. (Bob) 35
MacKechnie, Hugh 51
McCurdy, John A.D. 35

McLaughlin, Johnny 127
Molson, Ken M. 163, 179
Muraszew, Dr. A. 123
Page, Bette 163
Page, Ron D. 163
Pearkes V.C., Honourable George R. 35
Pedden, Murray 179
Perkins, Dr. Courtland 157
Plant, J.L. 141
Potocki, W. (Spud) 48-49, 51, 59, 71-72, 77, 83, 88-90, 93, 95, 113-116, 119
Rogers, Don vii, 71, 113, 150
Ronaason, Norm 72
Rose, Rodney 164
Shaw, Kate E. 179
Stewart, Greig 179
Thompson, D.L. 139
Westall, Eric A. 164
Woodman, F/Lt. Jack 56, 59, 71-72, 77, 93, 113, 115-116, 119, 149
Zurakowski, Jan 45, 47-49, 51, 55, 59, 63, 65-66, 71-72, 77, 85, 113-116, 119, 149-150

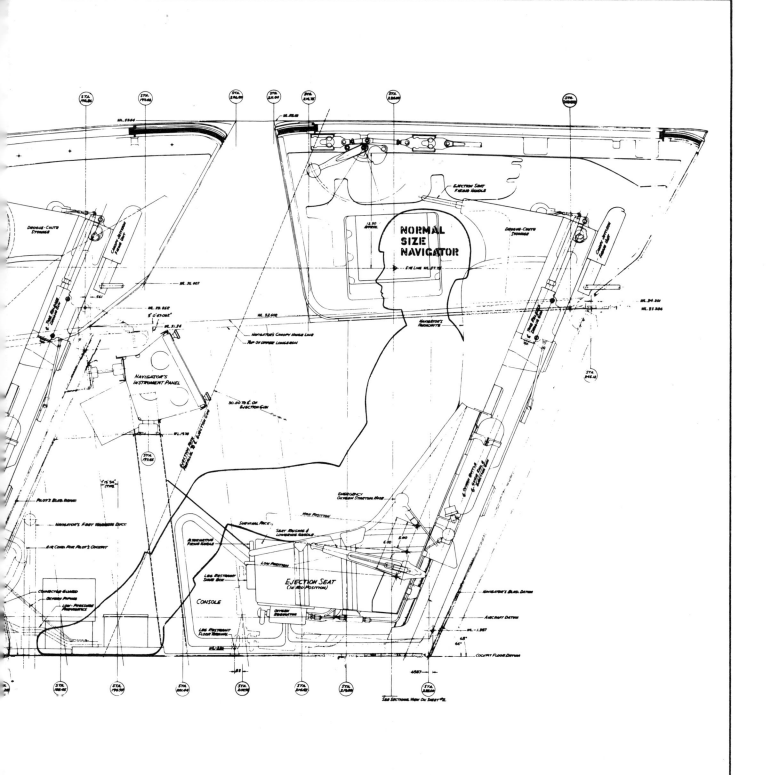

NORMAL
SIZE
NAVIGATOR

EJECTION SEAT
(IN MID POSITION)

CONSOLE

AVRO AIRCRAFT LIMITED
MILTON   ONTARIO

GENERAL ARRANGEMENT
PILOT'S & NAVIGATOR'S POSITIONS
FRONT FUSE

7-4452-7

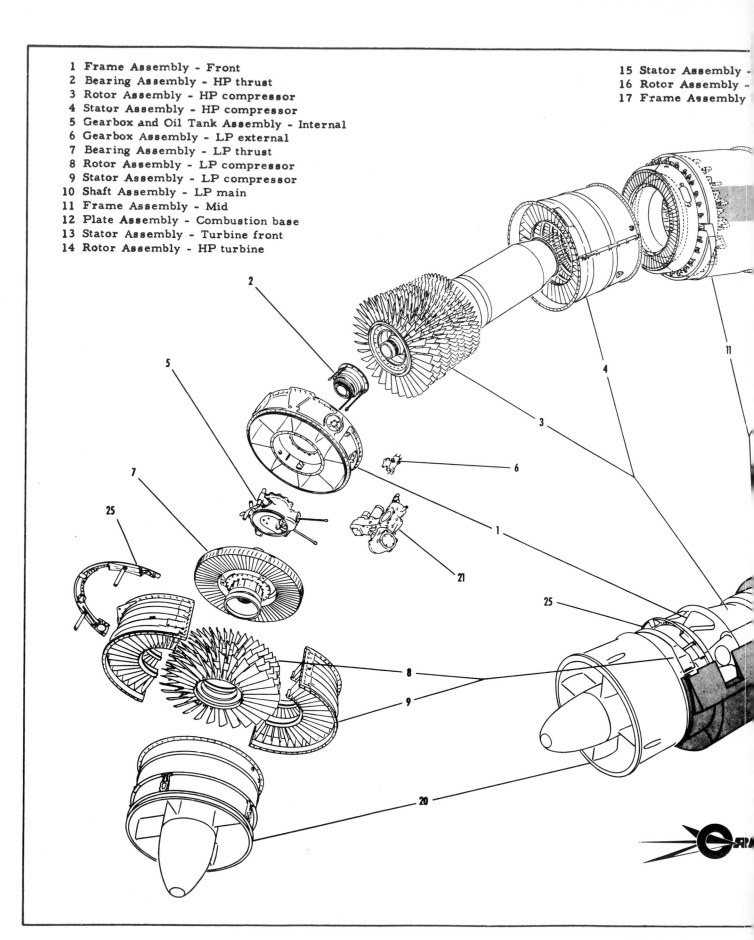

1 Frame Assembly - Front
2 Bearing Assembly - HP thrust
3 Rotor Assembly - HP compressor
4 Stator Assembly - HP compressor
5 Gearbox and Oil Tank Assembly - Internal
6 Gearbox Assembly - LP external
7 Bearing Assembly - LP thrust
8 Rotor Assembly - LP compressor
9 Stator Assembly - LP compressor
10 Shaft Assembly - LP main
11 Frame Assembly - Mid
12 Plate Assembly - Combustion base
13 Stator Assembly - Turbine front
14 Rotor Assembly - HP turbine

15 Stator Assembly -
16 Rotor Assembly -
17 Frame Assembly

Engine General A

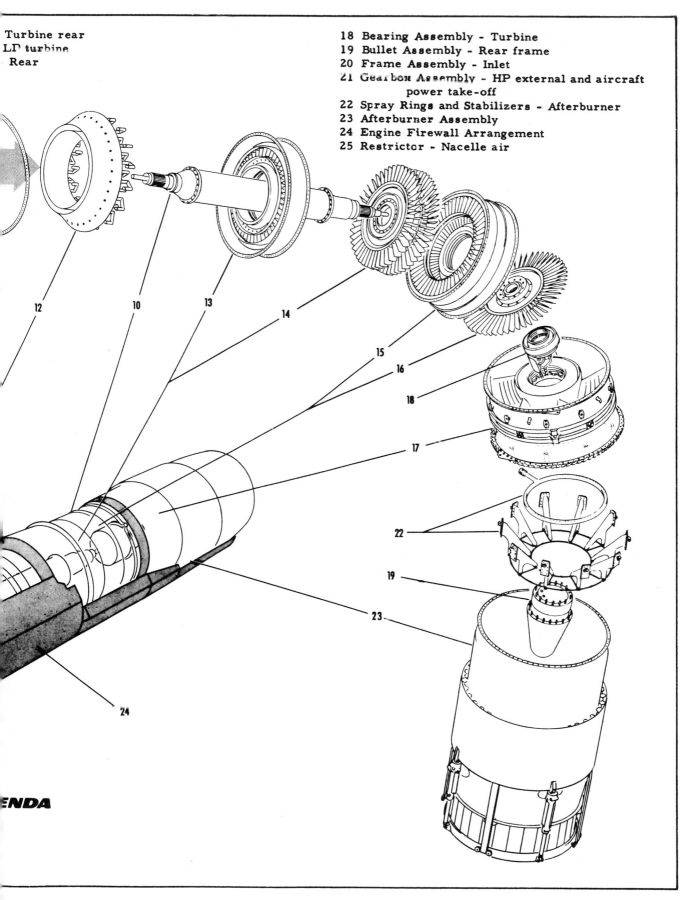

Turbine rear
LP turbine
  Rear

18 Bearing Assembly - Turbine
19 Bullet Assembly - Rear frame
20 Frame Assembly - Inlet
21 Gearbox Assembly - HP external and aircraft
      power take-off
22 Spray Rings and Stabilizers - Afterburner
23 Afterburner Assembly
24 Engine Firewall Arrangement
25 Restrictor - Nacelle air

ENDA

ssembly

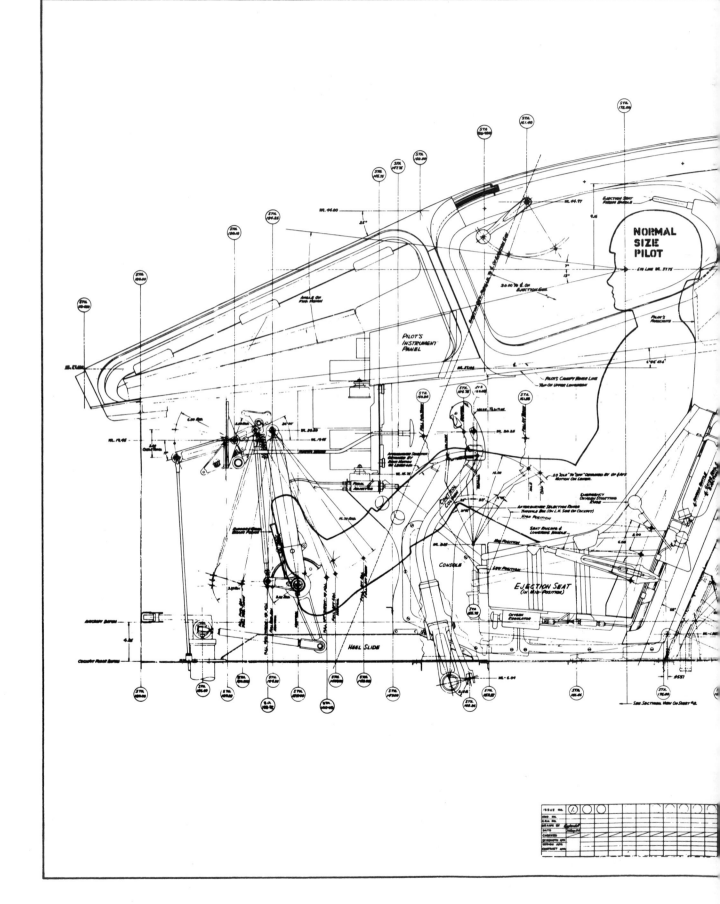